Texans ☆

THE TEXIANS AND THE TEXANS

A series dealing with the many peoples who have contributed to the history and heritage of Texas. Now in print:

Pamphlets — *The Afro-American Texans, The Anglo-American Texans, The Belgian Texans, The Chinese Texans, The Czech Texans, The German Texans, The Greek Texans, The Indian Texans, The Italian Texans, The Jewish Texans, The Lebanese Texans and the Syrian Texans, The Mexican Texans, Los Tejanos Mexicanos* (in Spanish), *The Norwegian Texans, The Spanish Texans* and *The Swiss Texans.*

Books — *The Danish Texans, The English Texans, The German Texans, The Irish Texans, The Japanese Texans, The Polish Texans* and *The Wendish Texans.*

The Melting Pot: Ethnic Cuisine in Texas — Historic overviews and recipes from 27 ethnic groups.

STORIES FOR YOUNG READERS

Designed specifically for school-age readers, containing historical fact, interesting information and dynamic accounts of people in Texas history:

With Domingo Leal in San Antonio, 1734; Who Are the Chinese Texans?; Our Mexican Ancestors; and *A Personal History: The Afro-American Texans.*

Texans ☆

• A Story of Texan Cultures for Young People •

Barbara Evans Stanush

1988

Texans: A Story of Texan Cultures for Young People
by Barbara Evans Stanush

John R. McGiffert, Executive Director

Production Staff: Jim Cosgrove, designer; Sandra Hodsdon Carr; David Haynes; Meredith Rees

Library of Congress Catalog Card Number 88-50983
International Standard Book Number 0-86701-040-1

First Edition

This publication was made possible in part by the Houston Endowment, Inc., and the Scurlock Foundation of Houston

Printed in the United States of America

Contents

Texans

JUST WHAT IS A TEXAN? That's a big question, as big as the state of Texas. Maybe it is better to ask "Who are Texans?" There are all kinds of Texans. Do you know any Vietnamese Texans from Houston? Do you know any German Texans from Fredericksburg? Do you know any Afro-American Texans from Palestine? Many different people have helped make Texas what it is today.

There were the first Texans, who lived here for thousands of years and left their stories painted on rock walls. There were explorers, who drew maps and named rivers. There were pioneers, who came in covered wagons and wrote diaries about their journeys. Many Texans came here from other countries. They told the stories of their lives, in many different languages, to their children and grandchildren. All of these people, and their stories, are part of our history.

You will meet many of these Texans in this book. People from all over the state have shared their stories. You will learn about their foods and their feelings, their work and their play, and much more. These ways of living are what we call "culture." Here you will discover bits and pieces of 15 Texan cultures. These are just a few of the many cultures in Texas.

What kind of a Texan are you?

Immigration

Moving and Meeting

MANY THOUSANDS OF YEARS AGO, people from Asia came to North America. Then, little by little, they moved south through the Americas. Some of these early people came in small groups to what is now Texas. Since then, people have moved to Texas from all directions, from all over the world. Texas is a meeting place.

When we move, we learn. Moving from one place to another, even just from home to school, we bring along our own ways and learn those of other people. We get new ideas. Children share their games, their jokes, and their jump rope rhymes. Grown-ups share their foods, their arts, and their ways of building houses and towns.

New ideas help us grow. We learn to enjoy new ways of doing all kinds of things. We learn to live together and share our different customs.

Why People Came to Texas

PEOPLE CAME TO TEXAS for many reasons. Perhaps they wanted land. Perhaps they wanted the freedom to live in their own way. Some may have been curious or looking for adventure. Others may have been fleeing from troubles.

These people were strong and willing to take risks. It was not easy to leave their homes and friends. However, they hoped to make a better life for themselves and their families in Texas.

How People Came to Texas

THE FIRST PEOPLE walked to get here. There were no wheels, no wagons, no horses. Some people may have ridden on a log down a river, but mostly they walked and walked and walked.

Much later, settlers came overland in wagons pulled by oxen or horses or mules. Many wrote about their journeys in letters and diaries. Others told their stories to children and friends. A grandfather described a trip he took when he was a boy.

"That's back there in history. . . . We didn't have cars or trucks. . . . Everything was wagons then, wagons and buggies. . . . Every night when we got to camp, Papa had to stretch up a tent, a little tent. . . . Some of us slept underneath the wagon."

In the 1800's, immigrants came from other countries on sailing ships. Journeys often took seven or eight weeks. Sometimes the wind stopped blowing, and the ship rocked on the ocean in the hot sun. At other times, the sea was so rough that it caused terrible seasickness. Passengers were crowded below the decks. Sometimes their food spoiled. Seawater often soaked their beds and clothes. There were also some good times, though, when the nights were clear. Then people sang or danced on the decks.

Many years ago, a Norwegian girl crossed the ocean to America. Later, in Oslo, Texas, she wrote about the trip.

> We left Haugesund about 4 o'clock in the morning. . . . Early that morning people sat along the mountain cliffs waving handkerchiefs.
>
> . . . One day [it was so rough] they put the ropes across the deck. We were so much used to the sea that we did not mind it. That day there was so much seasickness down below it was impossible to be there, so I sat and crocheted all day in the stairway leading up to the deck so I could feel the fresh air.

Many people are still moving to Texas. Some come by bus or by truck or car, pulling trailers behind. Others travel on railroads. Still others, from far away, fly into one of the international airports. Every year, thousands of newcomers make their homes in Texas.

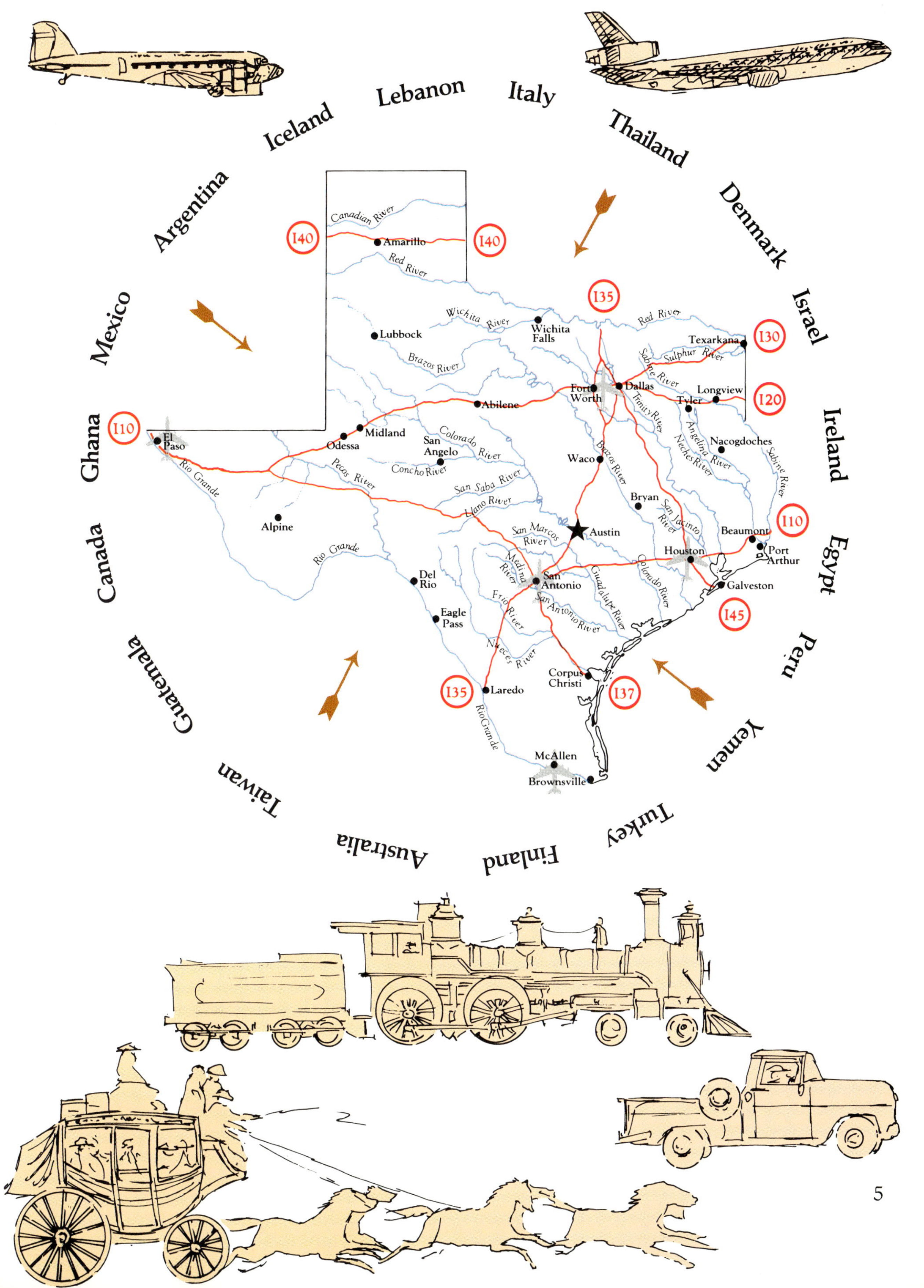
Lebanon
Italy
Iceland
Thailand
Argentina
Denmark
Mexico
Israel
Ghana
Ireland
Canada
Egypt
Guatemala
Peru
Taiwan
Yemen
Australia
Finland
Turkey
I40
I35
I30
I20
I10
I45
I37
Canadian River
Amarillo
Red River
Wichita River
Wichita Falls
Lubbock
Brazos River
Texarkana
Sulphur River
Sabine River
Fort Worth
Dallas
Longview
Tyler
Trinity River
Abilene
Midland
Odessa
El Paso
San Angelo
Colorado River
Concho River
Pecos River
Angelina River
Neches River
Nacogdoches
Sabine River
Waco
Brazos River
Rio Grande
San Saba River
Llano River
Alpine
Bryan
San Jacinto River
Austin
San Marcos River
Beaumont
Port Arthur
Houston
Rio Grande
Del Rio
Medina River
San Antonio
Colorado River
Galveston
Guadalupe River
Frio River
San Antonio River
Eagle Pass
Nueces River
Corpus Christi
Laredo
Rio Grande
McAllen
Brownsville

Indian Texans

INDIANS HAVE LIVED IN TEXAS for thousands of years. The earliest people of Texas moved from place to place, following large animals which they killed for food.

Later people hunted smaller animals and also gathered nuts, seeds, berries, and plants. They did not travel as much. Some of them lived in rock shelters high above the rivers. Others lived at the edges of the plains near streams or water holes. They learned to weave fiber from plants into baskets and sandals and mats. These Indians lived for several thousand years in this way.

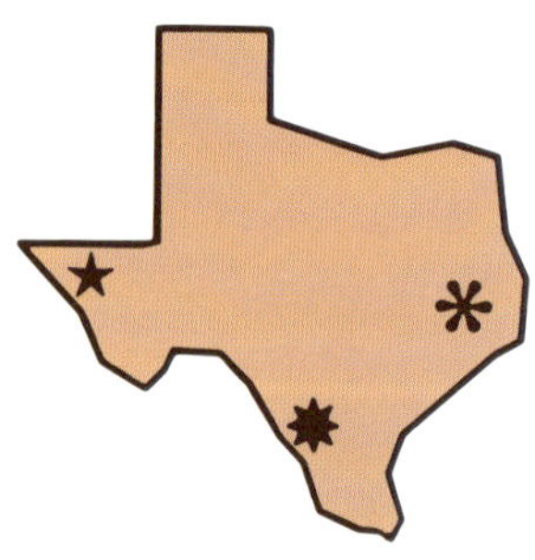

Kickapoos
Alabama-Coushatta
Tigua

Many different groups of Indians lived in Texas. When people from Europe and the United States came here, they settled on Indian lands. Many Indians died from diseases brought by these settlers. Others were killed in battles. It became harder for the Indians to hunt for food because settlers kept moving west. Most Indians left or were removed from Texas by the 1860's.

Today, three small groups of Indians live on reservations in Texas. They are the Tiguas, the Alabama-Coushattas, and the Kickapoos. Most Indian Texans live in cities, away from their tribes. Many of these people have come from other states to live in Texas.

Learning about Indians

HAVE YOU EVER held an arrow point in your hand? Have you seen a stone ax in a museum? Perhaps these objects were made by early Texas Indians. They did not have a written language, so they left no written records. However, they did leave behind objects that they made. We can learn from these objects.

Today scientists, called archaeologists, are carefully digging in the ground. They sift the earth searching for clues to Indian ways of life. The scientists find stone tools, pieces of pots, and bones and shells. They find pictures painted on rocks. They study these objects to help them learn more about Indians.

Indians knew how to live in the wilderness. They made tools from rocks and sticks. From plants they made medicines, and from animal skins they made clothing. Some of them made pots from earth.

Indian farmers grew many food plants that we eat today. Corn, beans, squash, and pumpkins are some of these plants.

We want to learn more about Indians. We can learn by doing what the Indians did.

Make a Grinding Tool

Find a flat rock. You will also need a smaller, round rock that you can hold easily. Put some seeds, like rice or grass seeds, on the flat rock. Roll and push the round rock over and over the seeds. Soon you will have a powder, called meal.

The Indians used stones to grind up nuts and seeds for food. They also ground up leaves and roots and seeds to make medicines. They even made paint by grinding pieces of colored rock and mixing this powder with water or animal fat.

Early Indian Paintings

LONG AGO, INDIANS PAINTED PICTURES on rocks. They painted on the walls of rock shelters and cliffs. They also painted designs on small river pebbles. There are many paintings on the walls of rock shelters near the lower Pecos River in southwest Texas.

These pictures tell us about early Indian life in Texas. There are deer with spears in their sides. There are huge panthers. Some pictures show tall men. One is 16 feet high. How do you think Indian artists painted these tall figures?

Scientists are studying these pictures. Some scientists think that the tall men were shamans. Shamans were medicine men, who cured sick people. In a few pictures, the shamans had round objects hanging from their arms. What were they? A scientist sifted the earth near a painting and found small bags made of cactus pads. Now the scientists had some clues. Perhaps the shamans carried bags made out of cactus pads.

What do you think the shamans carried in these bags? This is one of the questions that scientists are trying to answer.

It is sad that people have destroyed some of the paintings. They are thousands of years old.

Paint like the Indians

Find some smooth, flat pebbles. Paint some Indian designs on them or make up pictures of your own.

Many Different Indians

Coahuiltecans, Karankawas,
Lipan Apaches and Tonkawas,
Comanches, Kiowas, and Kiowa Apaches,
Jumanos, Wichitas,
Atakapans, and Caddos.

These groups of Indians lived in Texas when the early settlers came. The customs of these groups were as different as their names. They spoke different languages. Some groups moved from place to place, gathering nuts and berries and hunting animals for food. They lived in small camps and made shelters out of brush and animal hides.

The Indians who lived on the plains hunted buffaloes. They carried their homes, called tipis, with them. Still other Indians lived on the desert in houses made of sun-baked mud. The Caddo Indians in east Texas planted crops of corn and beans. They lived in villages near their fields.

A Caddo House-Raising

CADDO HOMES WERE very large. Some of them were more than 40 feet high. They were made of wood poles covered with long grasses, so they looked like haystacks. It took many people working together to build a Caddo home. They usually built one in less than a day!

A happy feast followed the work. At the beginning of the meal, men blew puffs of smoke from a pottery pipe, up, down, and to both sides. Then the workers ate deer meat, with corn served in pottery dishes. They had a good reason to celebrate. They had built a home for several families.

Cook Corn Soup

Here is an Indian dish that might taste like the Caddo meal. However, beef and bacon are used instead of deer meat. You can find shelled dried corn at a feed store. You can soak the kernels just like the Indians did.

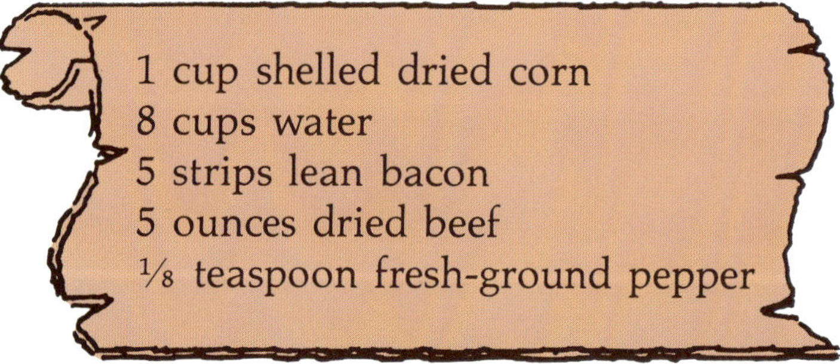

1 cup shelled dried corn
8 cups water
5 strips lean bacon
5 ounces dried beef
⅛ teaspoon fresh-ground pepper

Wash the corn. Soak it in 2 cups of water for 48 hours. Place the corn and the soaking water in a large pan. Add the other 6 cups of water and the bacon. Simmer, with the lid on, for 4 or more hours, until the corn is tender. Mix in the dried beef and pepper. Simmer, while stirring, for 10 minutes. Serve hot. This recipe makes 6 large servings or 30 tastes.

The Alabama-Coushattas

THE ALABAMA AND THE COUSHATTA INDIANS came from Louisiana to east Texas in the early 1800's. They built log houses and grew corn in their gardens.

Green Corn Ceremony

Long ago, the lives of these Indians depended on corn. Each summer, when the corn was ripe, the Indians celebrated for many days. First they cleaned their houses and made new clothes and pots. They ate up the last of the old corn. Then they did not eat any food for one or two days. Finally they feasted on the new green corn and gave thanks to the Great Spirit. They sang and danced in a circle to the shaking of rattles.

Sing to a Corn Dance Song

This song does not have words. Have someone play the notes. Make up syllables like "ah-ee" and sing along. Keep time by clapping or by shaking a gourd rattle.

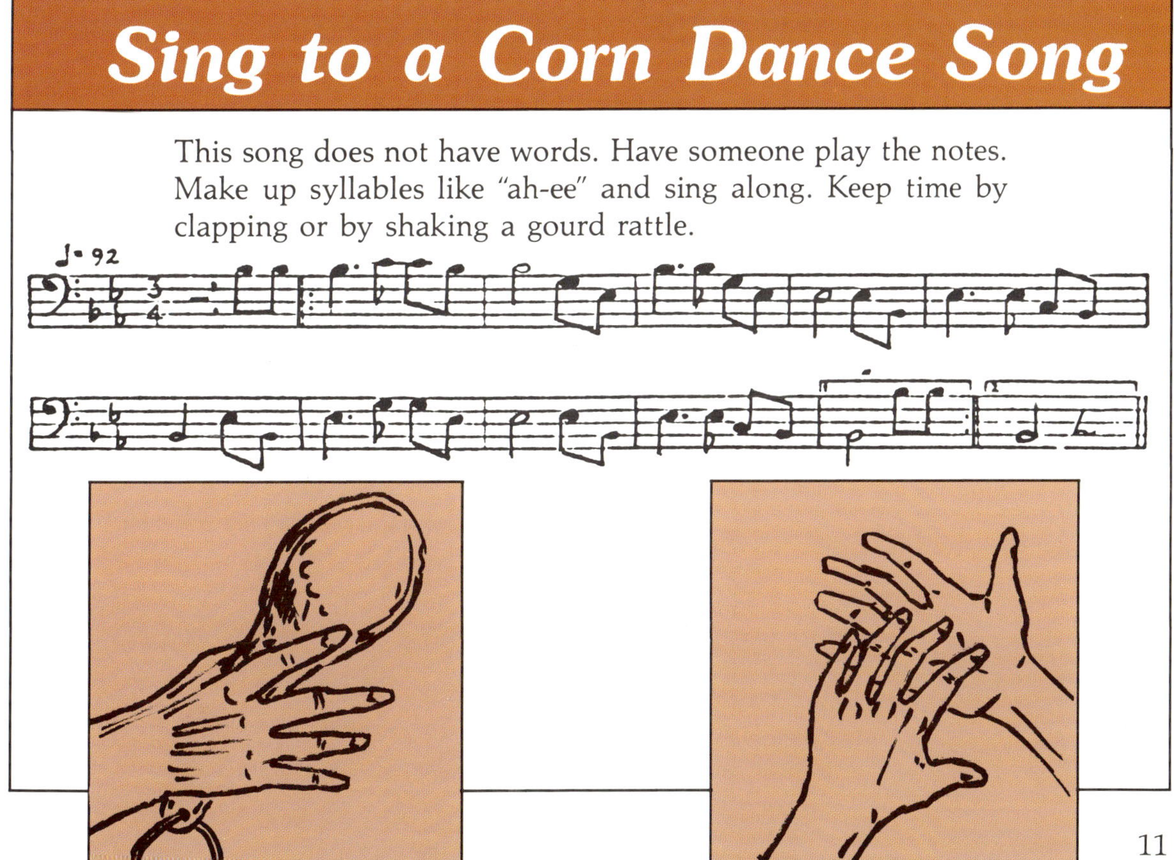

Today the Alabama and the Coushatta Indians live together on a reservation in the Big Thicket. Tall pine trees surround their brick houses. Many people still speak the Indian languages. Their leader is called a chief. Some of the grown-ups work in the lumber and oil businesses.

The children ride to school on a school bus. Baseball is one of their favorite sports. Their parents play baseball too.

The Tiguas

MORE THAN 300 YEARS AGO, the Tigua Indians came to west Texas from New Mexico. They came with Spanish priests, who had taught them the Spanish language and religion. Together they built a mission.

The Indians settled near the Rio Grande in the desert. They built homes of bricks made from adobe, a mixture of mud and dried grasses hardened in the sun. The Tiguas cooked outdoors in adobe ovens that looked like round beehives.

The Indians also built a church. They practiced their dances in the churchyard. Nearby they planted crops. They named their settlement Ysleta del Sur. This place is probably the oldest town in Texas.

Later a town named El Paso was founded nearby. As the town grew, it surrounded the Tigua church and houses. For many years, the Indians were forgotten. The Old Ones of the Tiguas did not forget, however. They kept their government, led by the chief. They guarded their drum with the sun painted on its head. They danced the old dances.

Today, the Tiguas are better known. They now have a reservation in El Paso, and many people visit them. These Indians still bake Tigua bread. The recipe is over 300 years old!

Many Indians live and work in cities. In Dallas, there are Indian organizations and Indian churches. There are classes and lectures about Indian culture. Indian Texans want to preserve their heritage.

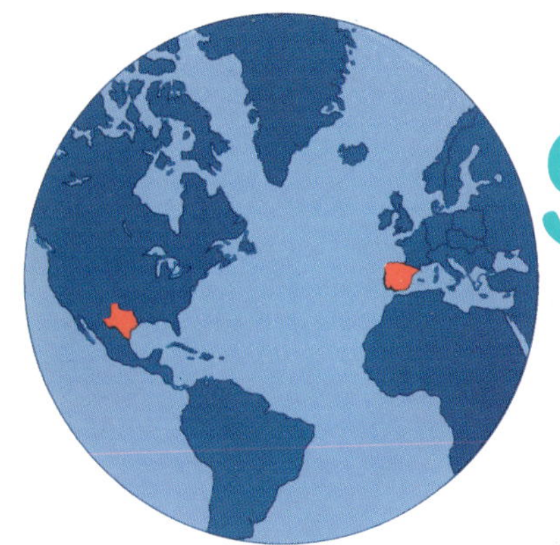

Spanish Texans

SPANISH EXPLORERS CAME TO AMERICA in the 1500's. They claimed this land for their king and called it New Spain. Texas was a wilderness in the northern part of New Spain. The Spanish government wanted to start settlements here.

Spanish Texans were people who settled Texas when it was part of New Spain. Most of the settlers came from what is now Mexico. They were descended from earlier Spanish settlers, Indians, and Blacks. Other settlers came from the Canary Islands.

For 300 years, much of America, including what is now Texas and Mexico, belonged to Spain.

Spanish Names and Records

THE SPANISH EXPLORERS WROTE about their travels in Texas. Spanish leaders kept good records. They drew maps and wrote journals about the land and the people. They gave Spanish names to rivers, places, plants, and animals.

Find Names on a Map

Look at a map of Texas. Find some towns and rivers with Spanish names. Many Spanish names end in *o* or *a, os* or *as.* Are there more Spanish names in some parts of Texas than in others? If so, can you guess why?

Neches Zavalla Aransas Medina La Reforma

Agua Dulce Del Rio Diablo Arroyo

A Spanish Gift

Mira, mi amigo,
Look, my friend,

Muchas palabras en español.
Many words in Spanish.

Amarillo, El Paso, Laredo,
Texas cities with Spanish names.

Rio Grande, Brazos, Hondo,
Texas rivers with Spanish names.

Agarita, armadillo, chaparral,
Texas wild with Spanish names.

Vaquero, lasso, bronco, corral,
Cowboy lore with Spanish names.

Lampasas, Lavaca, Llano, Frio,
41 counties with Spanish names—
And hundreds of Texas towns!

Calaveras Chico Aurora Zapata Santa Maria

Monte Alto Sierra Blanca Hidalgo

Spanish Pioneers

HOW DID SPANISH PIONEERS TRAVEL long ago? There were no superhighways. The explorers and pioneers had to clear paths through woods and brush. Sometimes they followed Indian trails.

People often traveled together in large groups called expeditions. The expeditions included soldiers, priests, animals, supplies, and sometimes families of soldiers. There were horses, cows, and pack mules. Sometimes there were also pigs, sheep, goats, and chickens. Food, equipment, and gunpowder were taken along. At times the animals wandered off, and everyone had to stop to round them up. The expeditions traveled only a few miles a day.

At night the expeditions camped near rivers, if possible, so as to have fresh water. There were no bridges across the rivers. Indian scouts often went ahead to make sure the group was going the right way. The path was sometimes hard to find.

People on each expedition kept journals. Part of one journal said:

> March 27, 1721. 9 Leagues. . . Due to . . . the fog . . . a soldier from the herd of horses was lost. His Lordship left two soldiers to search for him. We marched straight northeast for about two leagues to where we took a road over clear and level land. We had left the old road which was rugged and full of thickets. . . .

Missions and *Presidios*

SPANISH SOLDIERS AND PRIESTS traveled from Mexico to Texas to start settlements. The priests established missions for the Indians. They taught them the Christian religion and trained them to become good Spanish citizens. The soldiers established *presidios,* or forts, to protect the missions. The Indians were the workers for the Spaniards.

A Spanish priest wrote in his journal about the Indians at Mission San José.

> The Indian men occupy themselves with the work that is to be done. The old men make arrows for the soldiers; the young Indian women spin and untangle the wool and sew; the old women spend their time fishing in order that the priests may eat; the boys and girls go to school and pray in their turn.

The Indian children also helped with the work. The girls cleaned cotton before it was spun. Boys and girls spun cotton into thread. They helped the weavers, who wove the cotton and the wool into cloth. The boys also swept the patios and cleaned the stables.

Some Indians lived in the missions for many years. They learned to speak Spanish and were given Spanish names.

Other Indians left the missions. Most of the Indians in Texas did not want to live in missions. Some of them attacked the Spanish pioneers who were settling on lands where they had always lived.

A Spanish Town in Texas

IN 1718, AN EXPEDITION FROM MEXICO came to the San Antonio River. This expedition brought people to start a mission and a *presidio.* Later the Spanish government decided to send some settlers to establish a town nearby. The town was planned before the settlers arrived.

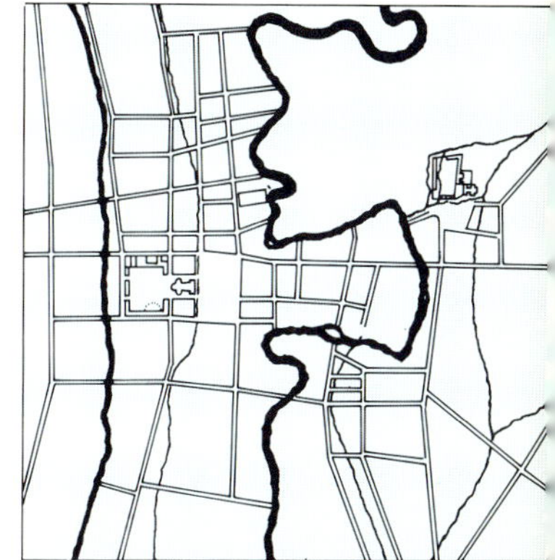
San Antonio, 1700's

The Spaniards planned towns carefully. First they looked for water. Water was needed for people, animals, and crops. They chose a place that was near a river or a lake.

Next the leaders made a map of the land. They planned where the *plaza,* or town square, and streets would be. They always made a *plaza* in the center of their towns. Then they drew a plan for canals which would bring water from the river to their homes and fields.

Finally the government asked families to come and settle. Settlers were given money, supplies, and free land. This is how the Spanish people from the Canary Islands came to live in San Antonio in 1731. They called their town Villa de San Fernando de Béjar.

Measure a Street

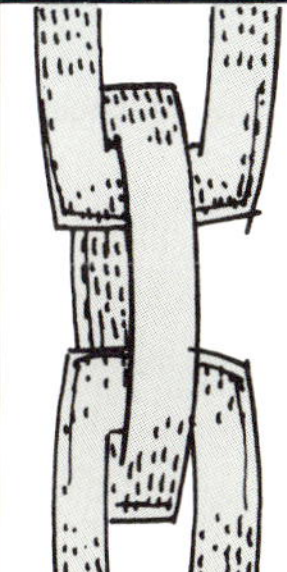

The first task for the settlers was to mark the places for the streets and the *plaza.* They measured with a long iron chain. The streets were 40 feet wide.

Measure a street near your home or your school to see how wide it is. (Be sure that there is no traffic when you measure!) Is it wider or narrower than a street in the Villa?

Life in the Villa

The houses of the Spanish settlers were small. The first ones were called *jacales.* They were made with upright poles plastered with mud. They had thatched roofs. Later people built houses of stone and adobe.

Families did not have much furniture. They had tables, cupboards, and chests. There were very few beds and chairs. They had *metates,* or grinding stones, and a few pots.

A widow in the Villa listed everything she owned in her will. She owned a stone house, cattle, some land for a farm, a ranch, and one day of water. That meant that she was allowed to use water from the canal to water her crops one day out of every 20 days. She also had 15 pictures of saints, a chest, a mattress, a quilt, a woolen skirt, and a branding iron.

A governor wrote about how people got their supplies.

> . . . All the buying and selling is done by trading. . . . Payments are made with fruit, chickens, eggs, and soap. Those who are better off pay with cattle and horses.

Laws were made to keep people healthy and safe. Some of these laws were:

- Everybody had to be inside their houses by 9 o'clock at night.
- Animals were not allowed to run loose in the town.
- No one could carry "short weapons," like knives.
- People who washed their clothes in the canals which brought drinking water would have the clothes taken away.

People spent most of their time at home or at work. Church bells announced important happenings, and they rang every night at 9 o'clock. Sometimes there were *fandangos,* or dances. The people had religious festivals, such as the Day of Corpus Christi. They called them *fiestas.* The people of the town exploded gunpowder to celebrate. On some holidays, young men raced each other on horseback.

Spanish Ranching

THERE WERE NO HORSES OR COWS in Texas when the Spaniards came. Spanish explorers brought these animals with them.

The missions kept herds of cattle. These herds were on land which was several miles from the missions. The priests trained Indians to take care of the cattle. Therefore, some of the first cowboys in Texas were Indians. They were called *vaqueros.*

The *vaqueros* had to round up the cows to count them and brand them. The mission ranches were very large, and they were not fenced. It was hard for the *vaqueros* to find the cattle, because the cows hid in the high, thorny bushes. The *vaqueros* of New Spain made lassos to rope the longhorns. They also made leather leggings, called chaps, to keep the horns and the thorns from sticking in their legs.

Here are some brands used in New Spain in the 1700's.

Juan Joseph Flores

Espada Mission

Luis Menchaca

Design a Brand

The Spaniards designed their brands. You can design a brand too. Mark your papers with it.

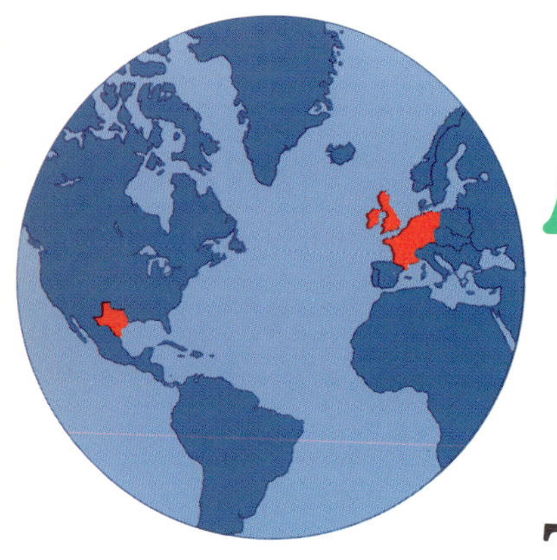

Anglo-American Texans

THE ANGLO-AMERICANS WERE people who moved from the United States to Texas. They spoke English. Their parents or ancestors had come from northern Europe to America.

Most of the Anglo-Americans did not come to Texas in large groups. Often families came alone. Many families traveled in covered wagons. Some of them tacked signs which said "G.T.T. – Gone to Texas" to the doors of the cabins they left.

Many Anglo-Americans came to east Texas in the early 1800's. They had heard about the cheap, fertile land and wanted to move to a new place. They built log cabins and cleared land for farms.

From Tennessee to Texas

ANN CAVITT TRAVELED TO TEXAS in covered wagons with her husband, Andrew, and their seven sons. She promised her parents to write in her journal every day. Sometimes she was so tired that she just wrote the date and number of miles they traveled. Here are some interesting parts of her journal:

> Dec. 6, 1834 . . . I was heavy-hearted for my own dear parents . . . but I have set my hands to the plow and shall not look back. . . .
>
> Dec. 12 . . . Andrew shot a tiny deer today, and we have enjoyed fresh meat, fried in the deep old skillet over the open fire. . . . We have made about 25 miles this week.
>
> Dec. 22 We arrived in Memphis today. . . . Victoria says she will wash in the big river if it ever stops raining long enough for the clothes to dry. . . .

Jan. 31, 1835 Today we got to the Red River, which Andrew declares is the sign to all people headed for Texas that they have arrived. . . . For the next two or three days the men will be cutting trees for making rafts. . . .

Feb. 5 . . . Our camp is snug. . . . The big fire is cheery. . . . I had never eaten fish cooked between hot rocks until now. . . . Andrew killed a mountain lion last night. . . . Little Sheridan was more frightened than the older three, but said stoutly, "When our Father kills a lion, he kills it dead, doesn't he?"

Keep a Journal

Write about a trip you have taken, or keep a journal on your next trip. Save your writing. It will tell people who aren't born yet about life in the 1980's and 1990's.

Life in a Dugout

LATER, MANY ANGLO-AMERICANS settled in north and west Texas. There were not many trees, so the settlers found other ways to make shelters. Their first homes were often dugouts, houses dug out of the side of a hill. Homes were far apart, sometimes miles from each other.

A woman told the story of her mother, who had built a dugout in the Panhandle.

> When . . . the wagon stopped, she felt so lonely. . . .
>
> The first summer Mama worked with shovel and pick to build the dugout. . . . Mama had her garden in, and she was plowing more land for corn when the first dust storm came up. The wind blew for three days so hard and the air was so full of dust that she had to tie a rope around her waist to get out to feed and milk the cow. . . .
>
> She had never heard sounds like was in the wind. She took to quilting all day every day. . . . There was nobody to talk to and nowhere to go to get away from the wind except underground.
>
> Mama's best quilts were her dugout quilts because that was when she really needed something pretty. . . . She made a Butterfly and a Dresden Plate and a Flower Basket during those two years in the dugout.

Quilts

PATCHWORK QUILTS ARE an American craft. Even cowboys on cattle drives used quilts, which they called soogans. They made bedrolls with them and carried them behind their saddles. The cowboys liked to crawl into their soogans on cold nights after a long ride.

Noah and the 4th of July

NOAH SMITHWICK WAS A BLACKSMITH from Tennessee. He helped plan a U.S. Independence Day celebration at Marble Falls in 1854.

The Planning Committee worked for weeks preparing for the party. Everyone from miles around was invited. The men built a huge shelter with poles and branches near the falls. Under this shelter, they set up a stage and lots of wooden benches for seats.

On the day of July 4th, people arrived on foot, on horseback, and by wagon. The program began with a blast of gunpowder from holes drilled in the rocks. That was the National Salute. Jabez Brown came next. He played "Yankee Doodle" on his fiddle. Everybody sang.

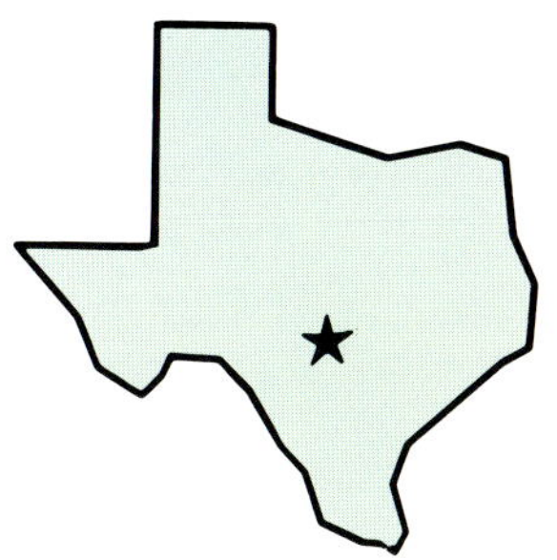

Marble Falls

Noah's 14-year-old son stood up. He had practiced his part for weeks with the schoolmaster. Now he read the Declaration of Independence. Then Dr. Moore, an orator, gave a long, long, long speech.

When the speech was over, everyone rushed to the tables. There were meats cooked over a fire, corn on the cob, and piles of vegetables. For dessert, there were watermelons, cakes, and wild berry pies.

Later a space was cleared for dancing. Jabez Brown climbed up on the stage and sawed away on his fiddle. He called directions for the dances too. Many people danced all night. In fact, some people didn't go home for several days.

"It was the greatest event the country had ever enjoyed," Noah Smithwick said.

Picture July 4th

There are no pictures of July 4th at Marble Falls. All we have is Noah Smithwick's story. Noah told his story to his daughter years later, and she wrote it down. Perhaps you can draw a picture from the story. You can add things too. The story didn't say what people did after that big dinner. Perhaps some people took naps. The women may have quilted. Did the children play games? Draw your version of the day.

A Texas Farm Boy

SILAS VANCE GREW UP on a farm near Fort Worth in the first years of the 1900's. He helped plant and chop and pick cotton. When there wasn't work in the fields, he cut firewood and milked the cows. He shelled corn and drew water out of the well to use in the house. Inside, he ground coffee and sliced bacon. Silas was glad to go to school to rest from his work.

His dad said, "Eat what is set before you." Silas ate. He ate hog liver, sauerkraut, turnips, cornbread, okra, buttermilk, black-eyed peas, and poke salad, a wild plant.

Life wasn't all work. On Sundays, Silas was "free as the wind." There were parties in the summer. The boys and girls played a running and swinging game called Snap. They went to summer church meetings too.

There were "singings" all year. People got together to sing church songs like "Shall We Gather at the River?" and "Little Brown Church in the Vale." They also sang songs like "Oh, Susanna" and "Dixie." Silas liked best the songs he and his brothers sang at home while they worked and played. Here's one.

"Old Dan Waggoner was a funny man,
Washed his face in a frying pan,
Combed his hair with a wagon wheel,
And died with a toothache in his heel."

The song had been "Old Dan Tucker," but the boys changed the name to Waggoner. Dan Waggoner was a rancher they knew.

“Make Do” and “Can Do”

THE EARLY SETTLERS had to "make do" with what they had or found around them. Many of them had spent all of their money to buy land and pay for their journey. They did not have money to buy houses, food, or clothes.

They built their homes with what they could find: trees, stones, river cane, sod, or mud. They got their food by hunting and picking berries and nuts. The children learned to spin and weave to help make cloth from cotton and wool. Almost everything was handmade.

The settlers became very good at creating tools and toys, clothes and new kinds of foods from what they had. They used everything. Scraps of cloth were made into quilts. Scraps of food were fed to the animals. "Waste not, want not," they said.

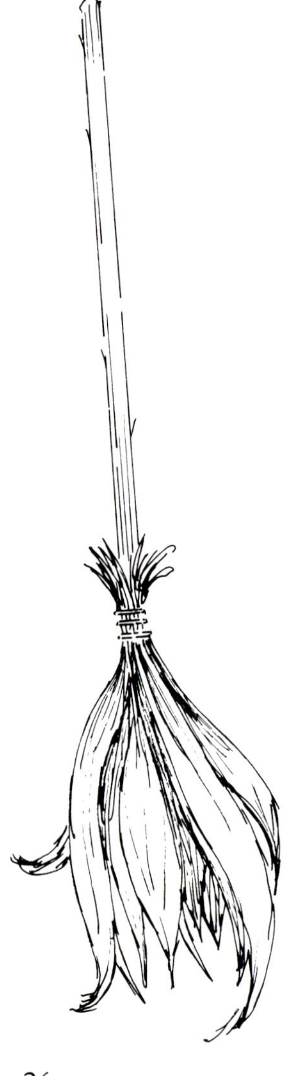

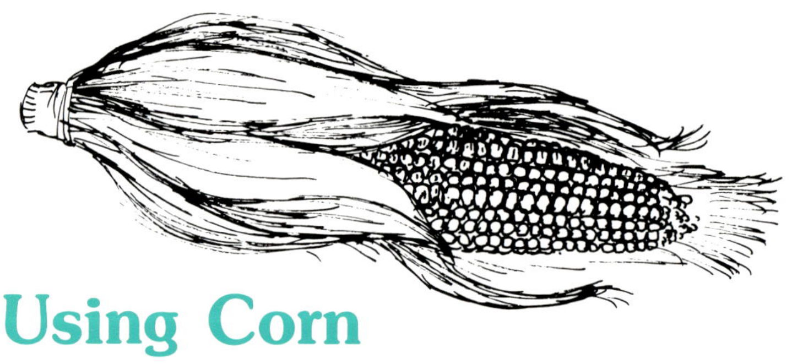

Using Corn

The settlers dug gardens and planted seeds for food. Corn was their main food crop. They used every part of the plant. Of course, they ate some of the corn and also fed some of it to the animals. They saved corn for winter by drying it. Dried corn was ground into meal and used for corn bread and other dishes. Corn shucks were used to stuff mattresses, to make mops, and to weave mats, baskets, and hats. Corncobs were burned for heat. Children made corn shuck dolls and used kernels of dried corn for game pieces. There were hundreds of uses for the corn plant.

Think like a Pioneer

Here are some objects that pioneers used. They used them in many different ways. Be creative like the pioneers. Think of more uses for these objects.

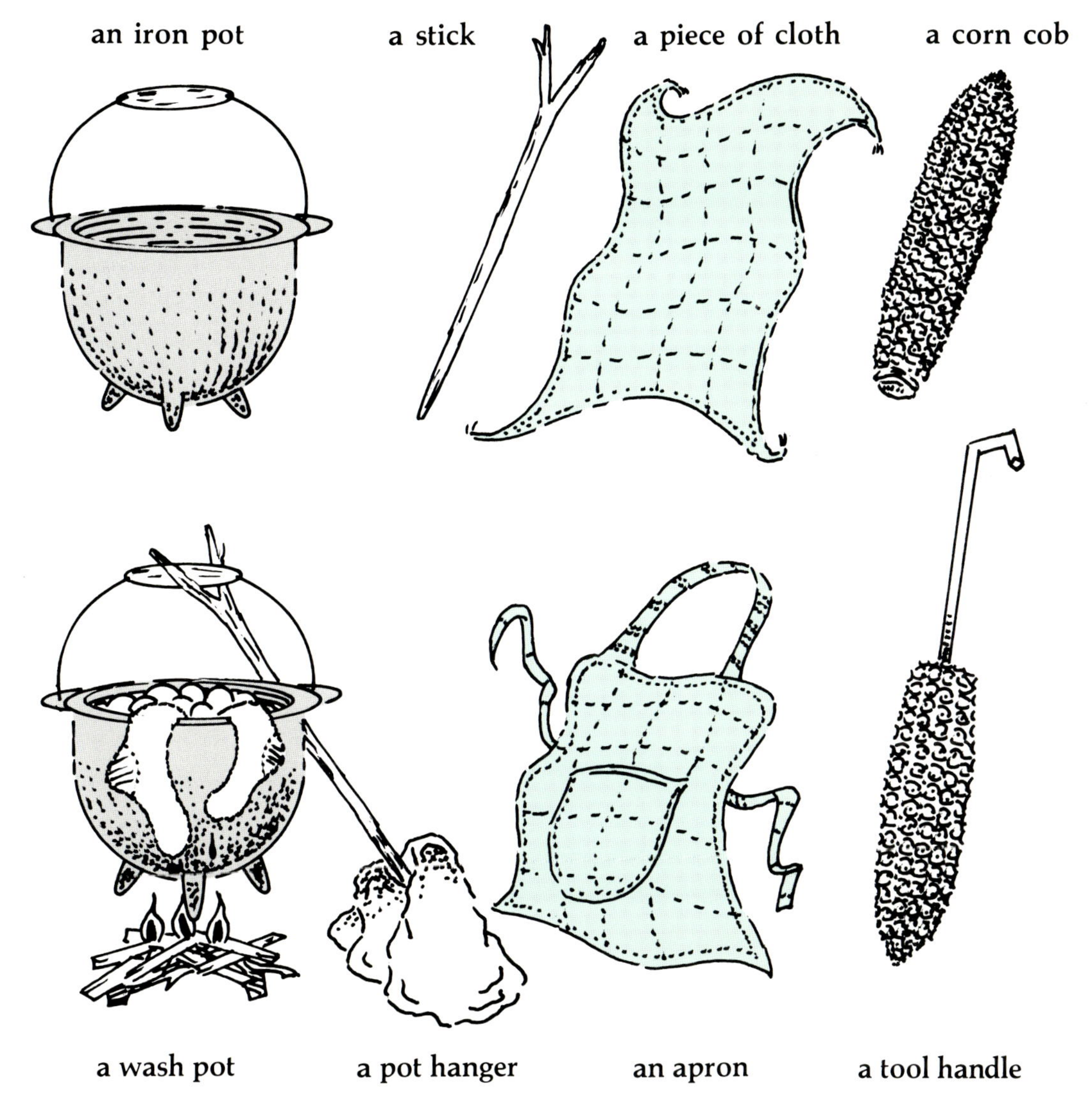

Afro-American Texans

AFRO-AMERICANS, OR BLACKS, are people whose ancestors came from Africa. Blacks have been in Texas for over 400 years. They lived in Texas when Texas belonged to Spain.

Many Blacks came to Texas as slaves. They were forced to work for no pay. They were not allowed to own land. Many were separated from their families. They were not free.

The slaves were given their freedom in 1865 after the Civil War. Life was still very hard for most of them, however. Many did not have any money, jobs, or homes. They were often not treated fairly.

For many years, Afro-Americans did not have the same rights as other Americans. They could not attend the same schools. They could not sit in certain parts of buses and trains. Blacks and other Americans thought that this was wrong. Together they worked to change the laws, so that all Americans would have the same rights. Now there are better laws, and Afro-Americans have many more opportunities.

Today, Black Texans are teachers, ministers, farmers and ranchers, lawyers, doctors, and government leaders. Others are business people, musicians and artists, and athletes.

Making Music

Long Ago

Black Texans told how they felt through songs. They sang at home and in church. They sang while they worked, to make life happier and to make the work easier. Often they made up the verses as they sang. Some even hid messages in their songs. "Steal Away to Jesus" might have meant "Come to the secret prayer meeting tonight."

In the 1800's, dances were sometimes held on Saturday nights. The musicians made their own instruments, like guitars and banjos. People clapped their hands and snapped their fingers to keep the rhythm. They danced many different kinds of dances.

New forms of American music were born from the folk music of Afro-Americans. They gave us spirituals, jazz, the blues, and ragtime.

Today

It is still a custom in many Black families to sing together. The Duckens family from Temple has been singing together for years. Now the 12 children are grown and live apart, but they still get together to sing.

Mrs. Duckens began their story. "The children started singing at home. They'd beat on the iron beds like a piano, pound a tub or bucket for drums, and use an old water hose for a horn."

Her son Bob said, "The only thing we knew was church. My brother Sylvester played the bed. He pretended it was a piano and made the sounds of the instrument with his mouth, and we sang like in church. My parents bought the piano from their old school for us. Sylvester never had a lesson. He taught himself to play the piano, and then he played the piano for the church."

"We started singing at Mt. Olive Baptist Church in Rogers, Texas. We have always sung together, and, when there were babies coming up, they just joined in," Mrs. Duckens said.

Try Out Some Music

Play some records of music by Afro-Americans. Tap out the rhythms of ragtime. (Scott Joplin, a Black Texan, was an inventor of modern ragtime.) Listen to a song by Huddie Ledbetter. Sing along with a spiritual. Dance to some jazz.

Story of a Cowboy

DANIEL WEBSTER WALLACE, "80 JOHN," was one of the many early Texas cowboys who were Blacks.

Webster, the Boy

Daniel Webster Wallace was born in 1860. His mother was a slave on a farm near Victoria. His only toy was a stick horse that she had made for him.

Webster worked when he was very young. He chopped the weeds out of the cotton fields. Later he plowed the fields. He attended school only a few days each year, when it was too cold to work. Webster's dream was to be a cowboy.

One day, when he was 15, Webster heard about a cattle drive. It was leaving for west Texas the next morning. He asked if he could go along.

"Can you ride?" the cattle driver asked. Webster said yes.

The man put him on a horse. The horse bucked, but Webster hung on. He got the job. Webster learned to ride, going up the trail.

"80 John," the Cowboy

When the cattle drive was over, Webster found other jobs. He worked for a rancher who had the 80 brand. Webster rounded up his calves and branded them with a hot iron. He did his work well, so the cowboys nicknamed him "80 John."

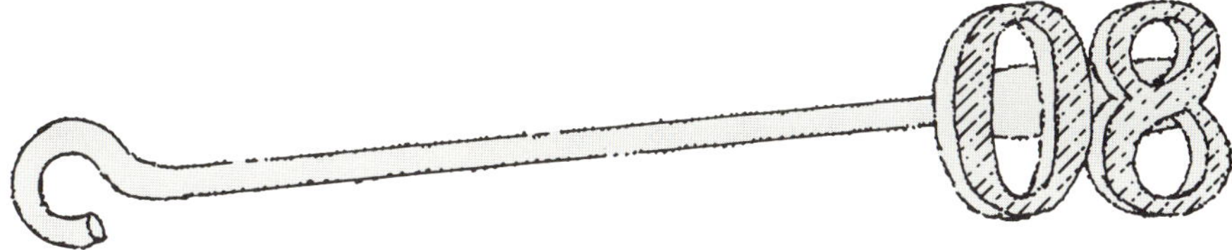

"80 John," the Rancher

Summer and winter, "80 John" worked as a cowboy. His dream grew. Now he wanted to be a rancher. That meant knowing how to read and keep records.

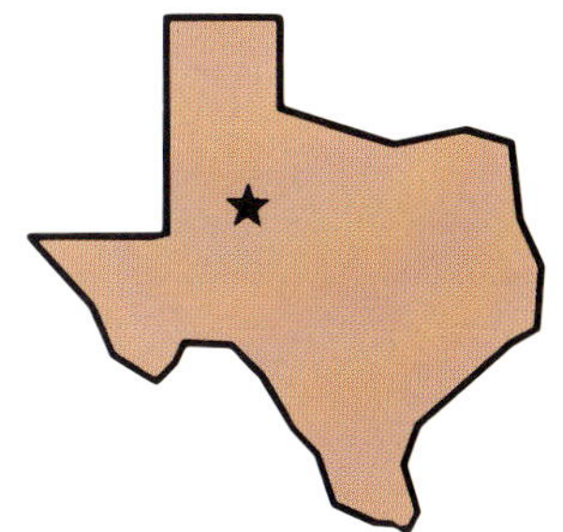

Colorado City

"80 John" went back to school. He was 25 years old and 6 feet 3 inches tall, and he started in the second grade. In two winters, he learned to read and write. He could also do fractions in his head.

"80 John" did become a rancher. His ranch covered 8,000 acres near Colorado City. He built one of the first windmills in west Texas on his land. He also paid for building a church in the town of Loraine.

Read about "80 John"

Hettye Wallace Branch wrote a book about her father. It is called *The Story of "80 John."* Learn more about Daniel Webster Wallace.

Mrs. Robinson and students of Markham School, 1933

Story of a Teacher

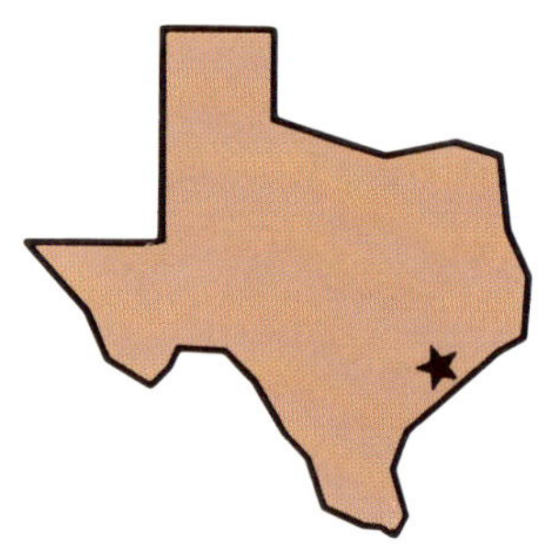

Markham

THE SCHOOLHOUSE HAD one room. Six windows supplied the light. There was no electricity. The teacher's desk was a table. Water came from a pump in the yard. This was Markham School, a country school at Markham near Bay City. Many Black children attended schools like this in the 1930's.

Mrs. Dorothy Redus Robinson was the teacher. She had more than 30 students. The youngest was six, and the oldest was 19. She taught eight grades.

"I prayed for this job," she said. "Jobs were scarce then." Mrs. Robinson started school with a box of chalk, a water bucket, and a dipper. These were her only school supplies.

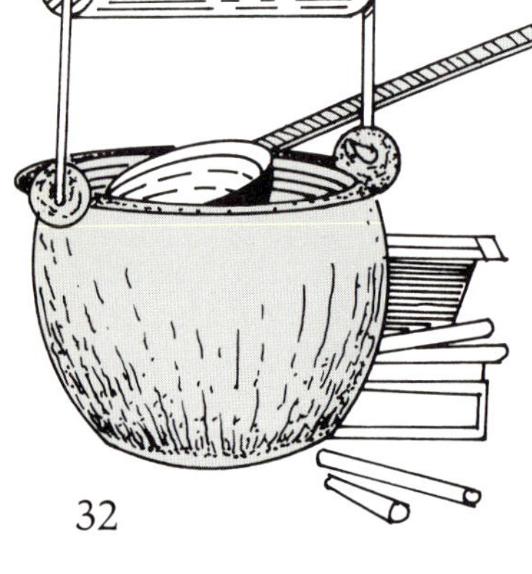

In School

The school day began with a prayer, then the flag salute and a patriotic song. Sometimes the children sang "Yes, Jesus Loves Me" and read verses from the Bible.

Mrs. Robinson created most of her teaching materials. She said, "I made charts from old window shades, and I used apple crates for bookcases. We played math games with nuts and kernels of corn."

Many children carried their lunches to school in syrup pails. They ate pork meat and biscuits with jelly. Sometimes they brought a baked yam.

Games at School

Mrs. Robinson talked about games like baseball and ring plays. "We played baseball all year. I made a string ball by winding and wrapping string. The bat was made from a tree limb. Everyone played. We just put them in the field.

"We had ring plays too, like 'Little Sally Walker.' The boys liked to play. They wanted to be in the center too."

Play a Circle Game

"Little Sally Walker" (**Directions**) Form a ring. "Sally" sits in the center. Sing or say the poem. "Sally" acts out the words. When she looks at someone, that person takes her place.

Little Sally Walker
Sitting in a saucer
Weeping in the morning
for her daughter.
Rise, Sally, rise,
Wipe your eyes.
Look to the East,
Look to the West,
And look to the one
You love the best.

Programs

There were lots of programs, and everyone in Markham came. February was the Month of Heroes. Mrs. Robinson said, "We always had a program then, with songs and speeches. Our heroes were George Washington, Abraham Lincoln, Frederick Douglass, Booker T. Washington and [Pierre] Toussaint L'Ouverture. Their pictures hung on the wall all year long. This was our connection with the great and the grand."

School Closing was the biggest day of the year. Everyone came in their new clothes. The children gave speeches and acted out plays. Everybody sang.

"The visitors clapped and clapped," Mrs. Robinson said. "The parents and children were prideful. Everybody was sorry when school was over."

Mrs. Robinson's class,
Rusk School,
Palestine, 1974

"Stories" of Children

CHILDREN HAVE CUSTOMS of their own, like playing games and saying rhymes. They play jump rope and ring games at recess. They also chant rhymes and keep time by clapping or stepping. Some of these playground rhymes are new. Others are hundreds of years old. They are passed on from one group of children to another.

Here are two rhymes chanted by children at St. James School in Houston. The first one is a jump rope rhyme.

Vaccination
Education
Does it hurt
Or does it sting
It don't hurt or anything.

Hey girl
Whatcha got
Soda pop
Gimme some
Uh-huh
Buy you some.

Hey brother
Whatcha got
Soda pop
Gimme some
Uh-huh
Buy you some.

(Hey sister, Hey mother, Hey uncle, etc.)

Two teachers collected these and other playground rhymes. You can read them in a book called *Apples on a Stick: The Folklore of Black Children.*

Do you chant some of these rhymes? Your rhymes may be a little different. Rhymes change when people tell them over and over.

Collect Neighborhood Rhymes

Think about the rhymes you say when you play. Do you remember jump rope rhymes, counting rhymes, nonsense rhymes, or hand-clap rhymes? There are also circle-game rhymes, teasing rhymes, and others. Ask your friends what rhymes they say. Collect these rhymes and put them into a little booklet. Give a copy to your school or neighborhood library. Send a copy to someone who lives in another city.

Did You Know?

JUNETEENTH, JUNE 19th, IS a Texas holiday. This was the day in 1865 that Black slaves learned they were free. Texans celebrate Juneteenth to honor their Afro-American heritage. In Houston, there is a big parade with floats and bands and dancers. Other towns celebrate with speeches, exhibits, picnics, and sports events. Is there a Juneteenth celebration in your town?

Mexican Texans

MEXICAN TEXANS have their roots in both Europe and America. They are descended from the early Spanish settlers and the Indian tribes of Mexico. Long ago, Texas was part of Mexico. Spanish, the language of Mexico, is spoken throughout the state, especially in south Texas.

Mexican foods, celebrations, arts, and clothing are part of life in Texas. There are Spanish-language newspapers as well as TV and radio stations. Many Texans speak two languages: English and Spanish.

The Neighborhood

LET'S VISIT A MEXICAN-TEXAN neighborhood in San Antonio and meet Rosa and Ramón. They live down the street from their school. There are lots of flowers and decorations in the yards along the street. There is a little shrine in one yard. The shrine contains a statue of Our Lady of Guadalupe. Inside some of the homes are altars. The altars are tables with candles, statues of saints, and religious pictures on them.

There are also some apartments in the neighborhood. Several years ago, teenagers painted a bright-colored mural about their history on the outside wall of an apartment building. Later, people in other neighborhoods began to paint murals too. Now there are more than 130 murals on walls in Mexican-Texan neighborhoods.

Rosa and her "Abuelita"

Rosa has eight people in her family: mother, father, four sisters, and grandmother. They all take care of each other. When Rosa started school, her older sisters peeked in the door of her classroom every day. Rosa is a good student. She reads well in both English and Spanish.

Rosa's face lights up when she sees her grandmother. She calls her "Abuelita" — Little Grandmother. Abuelita uses herbs, which are special plants, to cure illness in the family. She grows some herbs in the garden. When Rosa has a stomachache, her grandmother gives her *yerba buena,* or mint, tea to drink. When she gets sunburned, Abuelita rubs her skin with a piece of *zábila,* or aloe vera, to take the sting away. Abuelita buys other herbs at the neighborhood store. Rosa likes to go shopping with her mother and grandmother. The storekeeper often gives her candy for *pilón,* a little gift.

Ramón and the Low Riders

Ramón is a new student at school. He used to live up North, but his parents wanted to move back home to San Antonio. They missed their family and neighborhood. Ramón is glad that Wednesday is Mexican food day at this school. They didn't serve Mexican food at his other school.

Ramón loves cars, especially low riders. Low riders are older cars that are fixed up so that they ride low to the ground. They are painted with a bright-colored paint and are sometimes decorated with pictures. Ramón saw some low riders in the Mexican Independence Day parade on Guadalupe Street. He wishes he could ride in one.

Here is a poem Ramón's class composed at Halloween. Guess which lines Ramón made up.

Skeleton's Song

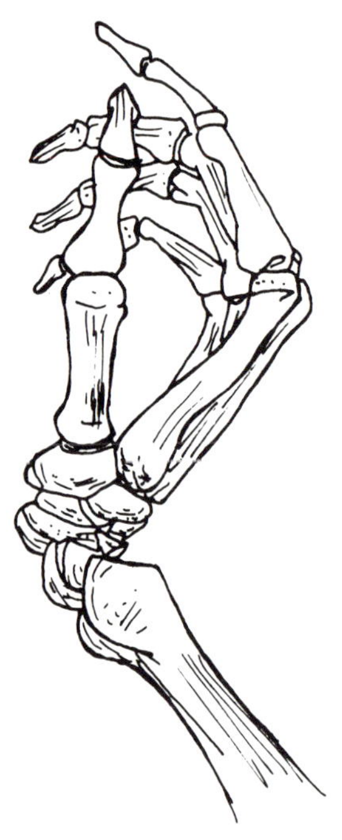

I am a skeleton.
I live in a coffin in the graveyard.
I stretch my bones on Halloween night.
I open the lid and creep out!

I slide in my bone-mobile,
a low-rider, a bone rider.
Dancing, wiggling,
jiggling my bones.

I twist the knob of my radio
and listen to the bone band.
Snapping my finger bones,
singing a bone song.

Boom! Bam! Bom!
You'll be doomed tonight at 12.

Holidays and Celebrations

HOLIDAYS AND CELEBRATIONS ARE PART of life in the neighborhood. There are *fiestas,* or festivals. There are plays and processions at church. At Christmastime, families make *tamales.* They wrap meat and *masa,* or corn dough, in corn shucks and steam them in a large can on the stove. At Easter, they make *cascarones,* colored eggshells filled with confetti. Rosa and Ramón love to crack the *cascarones* on their friends' heads. A few blocks from the school is the cemetery. People visit the cemetery on holidays and decorate the family graves.

Rio Grande City, 1985

El Día de los Muertos

The Day of the Dead is an important holiday for Mexican Texans. On this day, they honor the members of their families who have died. November 1st is the Day of All Saints. The next day, November 2nd, is the Day of the Dead.

During that week, the cemetery is bright with flowers and visitors. People stand outside the gates selling bunches of flowers. Flower shops across the street sell wreaths and bouquets. Families clean the graves and buy flowers to place on them. Sometimes they add a pumpkin, a balloon, or even a pinwheel. There is a service at the cemetery, and thousands of people attend.

San Antonio, 1985

Rio Grande City, 1985

Halloween

At school, the children celebrate Halloween. There is a parade. People from the neighborhood stand on the curb to watch the witches and cowboys, black cats and ghosts. Inside, the children draw pictures of crosses and skeletons. The skeletons dance and are merry.

Storytelling

RAMÓN'S CLASS WAS READING folktales. His teacher asked if anyone knew a storyteller. A boy raised his hand and said that his mother told stories. The class wanted to hear her stories, so Mrs. Mendoza came to class.

Mrs. Mendoza told little stories in Spanish. They were about birds and hermits, about mermaids and a weeping woman. She also told about growing up "en el rancho" (on a ranch) near Del Rio. The class loved the stories, so Mrs. Mendoza came back week after week.

Each day after she left, the students wrote down the stories in their own words and drew pictures. Later they made a book of the stories as a present for Mrs. Mendoza. They called the book *Los Cuentitos*—The Little Stories. One story was "La Sirena"—The Mermaid.

There was a girl. She would not pay attention to her mom. One day, when it was Easter Sunday, her mom told her not to go swimming. She did not pay any attention, and she went swimming. When she was going to get out of the water, she could not come out because she was half lady and half fish. She was a mermaid.

Find a Storyteller

Maybe your parents or grandparents have stories to tell. Find a storyteller and listen to her or his stories. You might want to record the stories of your family and other people in Texas.

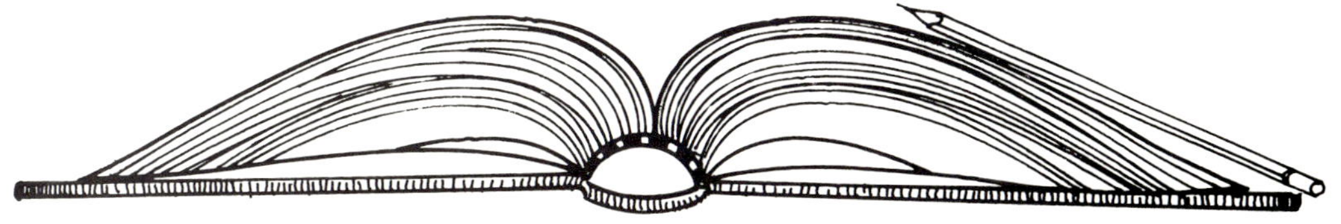

Birthdays!

CUMPLEAÑOS, OR BIRTHDAYS, ARE special. On Rosa's birthday, she gave favors to her classmates and to the teacher and the principal. Her sisters made the favors by fastening a pin to the back of a tiny card with Rosa's name and birthdate on it. They also tied a ribbon and a lollipop on each card. Lots of students at Rosa's school give favors on their birthdays. One day the principal wore three birthday pins.

Rosa has a party in her back yard on her birthday every year. Her father hangs a *piñata* in the tree, and her friends and family try to break it. The children can't wait to hit the large papier-mâché figure, which is covered with bright tissue paper and filled with candies. They take turns hitting it with a broomstick until it breaks. When the candies tumble out, the children scramble for them. Then everyone eats *tacos*, *tamales*, and *frijoles*, or pinto beans, and other foods. Of course, there's always a birthday cake.

Rosa dreams about her *quinceañera*, her 15th birthday. This is a special birthday for girls of Mexican heritage. It is the day they pass from girlhood to womanhood. Some girls have fancy ceremonies. Rosa dreams of wearing a long white dress and having 14 friends, one for each year of her life, in rainbow-colored dresses, as her attendants. There would be a service at church and a party afterwards. She knows that not everyone can have such a fancy *quinceañera*, but she can dream!

Families Who Make Music

MANY MEXICAN-TEXAN FAMILIES make music. Raymond McCumba III, an accordion player, grew up near Rosa and Ramón. He said, "My father played the accordion. When he set it down, I'd pick it up and start squeezing. . . . I was four years old. Now I have two sons, and the little one is always punching the buttons on my accordion. I hope he plays someday too." Raymond will teach him.

The Jimenez Family and Conjunto

The Jimenez family of San Antonio helped to invent a new kind of Texas music called *conjunto.* Today Flaco Jimenez plays *conjunto* music all over the world. He plays the accordion and sings in Spanish with his band.

It all started with his grandfather and the German Texans. Flaco said, "My grandfather used to go to the German dances in New Braunfels. He used to dance and see how that music was played . . . that oompah music. Then he managed to buy a button accordion. . . . He used to play German polkas. Then my father started playing in the 1930's after learning from my grandfather."

Flaco's father, Santiago, mixed polka music with Mexican folk songs. That music became *conjunto.* He made up new songs in Spanish. They were about everyday life. He taught his sons to play *conjunto* music too.

Flaco said, "He called me one day and said, 'Son, come over, because I've got a song here. Nowadays everybody is wearing blue jeans.' So he gave me that song, 'Pantalón Blue Jeans.'

"My dream was to play like my dad. . . . I caught on to what my father played, and I added a little more jazz."

Listen to Conjunto

Play a record of *conjunto* music. You'll hear Spanish songs with music that people like to dance to. The word *conjunto* means a getting-together of musicians. They usually play the accordion, the *bajo sexto* (a 12-string guitar), a bass, and drums.

German Texans

IN 1844, THREE SAILING SHIPS landed on the Texas coast. The ships were filled with hundreds of people from Germany. They had read about Texas in newspapers and letters and decided to move across the ocean. These people paid a German travel company for their trips and some land.

When the Germans arrived in Texas, there was no land ready for them. They had to wait on the coast all winter. It was rainy and cold, and there were no houses. They had to dig holes in the ground and cover them with branches and moss for shelter. Sickness spread through the group. Many people died.

Finally some land was found. The Germans followed a river from the coast to a place they called New Braunfels. It was a hard trip, and more people died. When they reached their land, the tired people began to build log cabins and plant seeds. Texas was not what they had expected.

New Braunfels grew, however. More Germans came to Texas. Soon the town of Fredericksburg was started.

Today, many German Texans still live in New Braunfels and Fredericksburg. They live in many other places too. German Texans are the fourth-largest group in Texas. They have kept many of their customs. There are singing groups and shooting clubs. They still have oompah bands and parades. Every spring and fall, there are festivals with German foods and dancing. People eat foods like sausage and sauerkraut and pumpernickel bread. They dance the polka to oompah music.

The First Day of School

THE GERMAN PIONEERS in New Braunfels wanted a school for their children. Most of the people lived in tents or grass huts at first. Only a few had log cabins, and there was no schoolhouse in 1845. However, there would be a school! Class would be held outside. The sky would be the roof. School would begin August 11th.

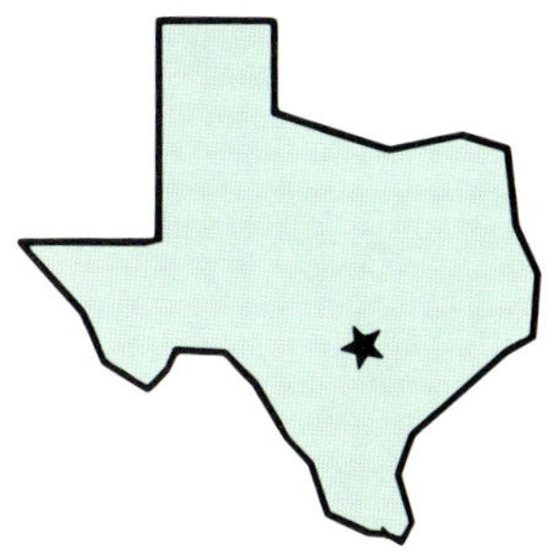

New Braunfels

At dawn on the 11th, the town's cannon boomed to wake everyone. Hermann Seele, the teacher, was already awake. Soon, people were busy carrying water from the river and cooking breakfast. Some were milking cows. At 6 a.m., a bell rang to call people to work.

Mr. Seele walked to a grassy place by some trees. This was the school. Fifteen children were waiting. *"Guten Morgen,* Herr Seele – Good morning, Mr. Seele," they greeted him and shook his hand. The smaller children sat down on the grass in front of their teacher. The older students used a bench.

The boys and girls were of all ages. Most of them were barefoot. They all spoke German. Many didn't know any English words yet.

The students would learn two languages, English and German. They would study arithmetic, reading, and nature.

A few children had slates that they had brought from Germany. Their slate pencils were made out of hard blue clay from the river bank. The students had made the pencils themselves. The other children had to do their math in their heads.

Maus,
mouse

Recess was at 8:00. The children had studied hard for two hours. Now they played hide-and-seek. They ate their corn bread and cold beef. For dessert, some children ate berries they picked from the bushes.

Soon the students were back at work. As the sun burned hotter, they moved into the shade. Mr. Seele stood against a tree to teach the last lesson. The children studied the trees, the plants, and the rocks at their feet. They didn't have a science book.

At 10:00, Mr. Seele took the youngest children by the hands. He led them back to their homes. School was over.

Hermann Seele never forgot his first day as a teacher. Many years later, he wrote a book and told about his feelings that day. When we read his story, it seems as if we were there.

Play with Words

German Texans liked to play with words. Mr. Seele's students probably told riddles and tongue twisters. Here are two that were spoken in the Texas Hill Country long ago. See if you can say the words in German.

A TONGUE TWISTER: ***Fischers Fritz fischt frische Fische:***
Frische Fische fischt Fischers Fritz.

Fisher's Fritz fishes fresh fish:
Fresh fish fishes Fisher's Fritz.

A RIDDLE: ***Was ist zwischen Berg und Tal?***
Antwort: Und.

What is between mountain and valley?
Answer: And.

A German-Texan Christmas

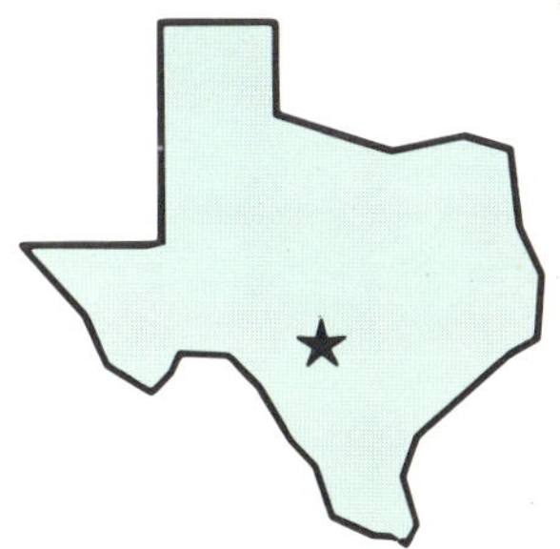

Fredericksburg

DID YOU KNOW THAT CHRISTMAS TREES were not always part of Christmas? The German people started this custom. Hundreds of years ago in Germany, people went into the forests and cut fir trees. They brought the trees into their homes and decorated them with candles and cookies.

When Germans came to Texas, they brought their Christmas customs with them. This is how a German family in Fredericksburg celebrated Christmas long ago. There were no fir trees in Texas, so they went out into the hills and cut a cedar. Cedar trees were evergreens and had a lovely smell.

The Christmas tree was placed in the best room in the house. The children did not help decorate the tree. It was to be a surprise. Their parents decorated it behind closed doors on December 24th. Christmas was celebrated that evening.

The children could hardly sit through supper. Father left the table early to light the wax candles on the Christmas tree. That was also the time Santa Claus came. He left presents under the tree. They were not wrapped.

Finally a little bell rang, which meant Santa had left. Father threw open the doors, and there was the tree, glowing with candlelight. A water bucket stood nearby in case of fire.

There were beautiful cookies on the tree. They were cut in the shapes of people, stars, and animals, and they were decorated with icing. There were nuts covered with silver paper and a few glass ornaments from Germany. Under the tree there were presents. Mother had knitted scarves, and Father had whittled toys. There was even a store-bought doll and a knife. The oranges and apples were special treats.

The children just stared for a minute. Then the whole family marched into the room. The littlest ones went first. They sang "Stille Nacht" – "Silent Night" as they entered. The Germans loved to sing, and Christmas was a time for singing. What a merry Christmas!

Try Some Christmas Customs

How do you celebrate Christmas? Why not add a custom or two? Cover nuts with aluminum foil, and bake some cookies to use as ornaments. Hang them on your tree.

German Sugar Cookies

½ CUP BUTTER
1 TEASPOON VANILLA
1 CUP SUGAR
1 ¾ CUP FLOUR
1 EGG
½ TEASPOON BAKING SODA
1 TEASPOON CREAM OF TARTAR

Directions

1. Mix butter and sugar together until creamy.
2. Add egg and vanilla, and beat until smooth.
3. Combine flour, baking soda, and cream of tartar. Stir into creamed mixture.
4. Chill dough at least one hour.
5. Turn on oven. Set at 350 degrees.
6. Roll out dough ¼ inch thick on waxed paper or a floured board.
7. Cut out with Christmas cookie cutters, and place on cookie sheets.
8. Bake about 10 minutes, until golden. While cookies are still warm, make a little hole in the top of each one.
9. Decorate the cookies with icing, sugar, and cinnamon, or with colored sugar.
10. When ready, put strings through the holes, tie in loops, and hang the cookies on the Christmas tree.

Kindermaskenball – A Children's Parade

IN THE SPRING, for more than a hundred years, the children of New Braunfels have had their own parade.

They parade in costumes through the town to the park, where they have a picnic. Policemen stop the traffic, and lots of people line up on the curb to watch the parade. First come the babies in strollers, pushed by their mothers. Next come the kindergarten and first grade children. The older ones follow. There are Indians and clowns, spacemen and pioneers. Everyone has balloons. The school bands play march music. All the band members wear costumes too.

This is an old German custom. The German people planned parades and dances just for children. Hermann Seele, the schoolteacher, started this custom in Texas in 1856. His students walked a mile and a half to a hall and then had a dance.

Laura Eiband remembered a *Kindermaskenball* in the early 1900's.

"My mother sewed from daylight to dark for weeks, so that we would have the prettiest costumes. We had a parade, and every child in school, almost, took part, and the kids danced all afternoon at the old opera house. That was the great thing of the year."

The word *Kindermaskenball* means children's masked dance in German. Today there is no dance, but the parade is still called *Kindermaskenball*. The German Texans keep their customs!

Polish Texans

DID YOU KNOW THAT THE FIRST Polish colony in the United States was in Texas? Polish immigrants settled at a place they called Panna Maria in 1854. Panna Maria is on the San Antonio River, not far from San Antonio.

Later, Polish people settled in Bandera, Thurber, White Deer, and other places. Most of them were farmers. However, the Poles who came to Thurber were coal miners.

Panna Maria

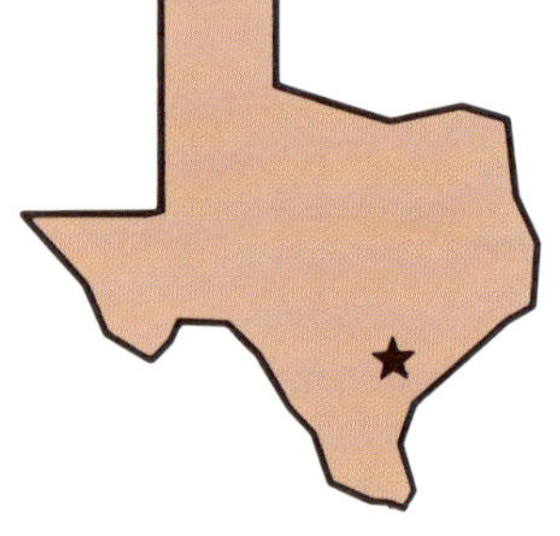

Panna Maria

PANNA MARIA IS STILL a little village. You can see an old white church and stone houses with steep roofs. These buildings were built by the immigrants. Many people in Panna Maria still speak Polish.

There is a huge live oak tree next to the church. The first settlers camped under that tree. It is still standing more than 100 years later. Now Polish people from all over the world come to Panna Maria to see it. There they also visit the oldest Polish church and the oldest Polish school in the United States.

Some people in Panna Maria know the stories of those first settlers. They heard the stories from their grandmothers. A lot of history is told by grandmothers. Here is what a Polish grandmother might have said about coming to Panna Maria.

A Grandmother's Story

From Poland to Texas

"A long time ago, we lived across the ocean in the Old Country. We were Polish, but Poland was not free. It was ruled by Germans and Russians and Austrians. The rulers didn't like us to speak Polish. One year, there was a bad flood. Food was scarce, and prices rose higher and higher. My children were lucky to get even an apple for a Christmas present.

"Then, there was a letter telling us to come to America, to Texas. Father Leopold Moczygemba had written the letter. He was a Polish priest who had gone to Texas. He said we could have more land there. We would have our own church, and we would be free.

"Many families wanted to go to Texas. We sold our land. The grandparents who stayed behind helped us to pay for the trip.

"We crossed the ocean to Texas on a sailing ship. It took all of October and November to reach land again. Many of us were seasick. Three people died on the ship, and we buried them in the ocean."

From the Coast to Panna Maria

"Finally our ship landed on the coast of Texas. My little Jasiek thought the meadows would be full of raisins waiting for him. There were no raisins, and no one met us. We put our things in oxcarts. We hadn't brought much, just our clothes, feather beds, a few tools, and a cross for a new church. We walked alongside the carts for many days until we met Father Leopold.

"People laughed at us because we didn't know English and because we looked different. Some of us had on wooden shoes. We wore black felt hats with broad brims and blue woolen jackets. Our skirts were two or three inches above our ankles. The Americans were surprised that our skirts were so short! Their women's skirts covered their ankles.

"We walked for three weeks from the coast to our land. We saw some wild cows with long horns along the way. There were rattlesnakes too. Oh, we were so scared of those snakes."

The End of the Journey

"At last we came to the land that Father Leopold had found for us. There was no church. There were no houses. The land was rough, and the grass was tall. There were some live oak trees at the top of the hill. That was all.

"The day was December 24th, Christmas Eve. We had our first Christmas Eve service at midnight under the biggest tree. We thanked God for bringing us here and asked Him to help us make a home in this wild, new country. We named this place Panna Maria."

Christmas Eve and the *Opłatek*

CHRISTMAS EVE IS AN IMPORTANT holiday for the Polish Texans.

A group of Polish Texans in San Antonio have a *Wigilia*, or Vigil, supper in early December. They invite people to come to the supper and learn about the Polish Christmas Eve customs. One custom is to share the *opłatek*. The *opłatek* is a wafer, a flat piece of bread, with a Christmas picture pressed into it. It is the size of a postcard.

The dinner begins after the first evening star appears in the sky. The *opłatek* is shared before the meal. A Polish Texan said, "My grandfather would break it in pieces and pass the pieces around to everyone."

All the guests at the dinner receive a piece of the *opłatek*. They each share their piece with the people sitting near them. They exchange good wishes, like "Peace be with you." Then they eat the bits that they have been given.

Some Polish Texans send little pieces of the *opłatek* in letters to friends who are far away. Even if there is only a tiny bit left, it can be shared.

Wycinanki – Paper Cuttings

PAPER CUTTING IS AN OLD Polish custom. Mrs. Gladys Moryl grew up in Lockhart. Her mother folded paper and cut it with scissors. Mrs. Moryl said, "My mother made flowers and little cut-out designs. She hung them up on the walls. She put them on the windows too, mostly on the windows." The paper cuttings were most often used to decorate for the holidays.

Mrs. Maria Garczynski has made hundreds of Polish paper cuttings. She said, "I used to make snowflakes and things like that when I was a child in Poland." Now she lives in Houston. She taught herself to make fancy Polish designs because she wanted to continue this custom. She wanted people to see the beautiful designs.

Mrs. Garczynski makes many different kinds of designs. Some are cut out of black paper and look like lace circles. Others have lots of pieces of different colors pasted on top of each other. One paper cutting has 300 pieces in it.

Make a Bookmark

Here is a bookmark which Mrs. Garczynski designed for you to use with this book. Cut a strip of black or colored paper 8 inches by 1½ inches. Fold it in half, and copy the design on one side of the fold. Cut out the design, cutting through both sides of the paper at once. Unfold the paper cutting, and paste it on a piece of white cardboard 8½ inches by 2 inches. Now you have a bookmark.

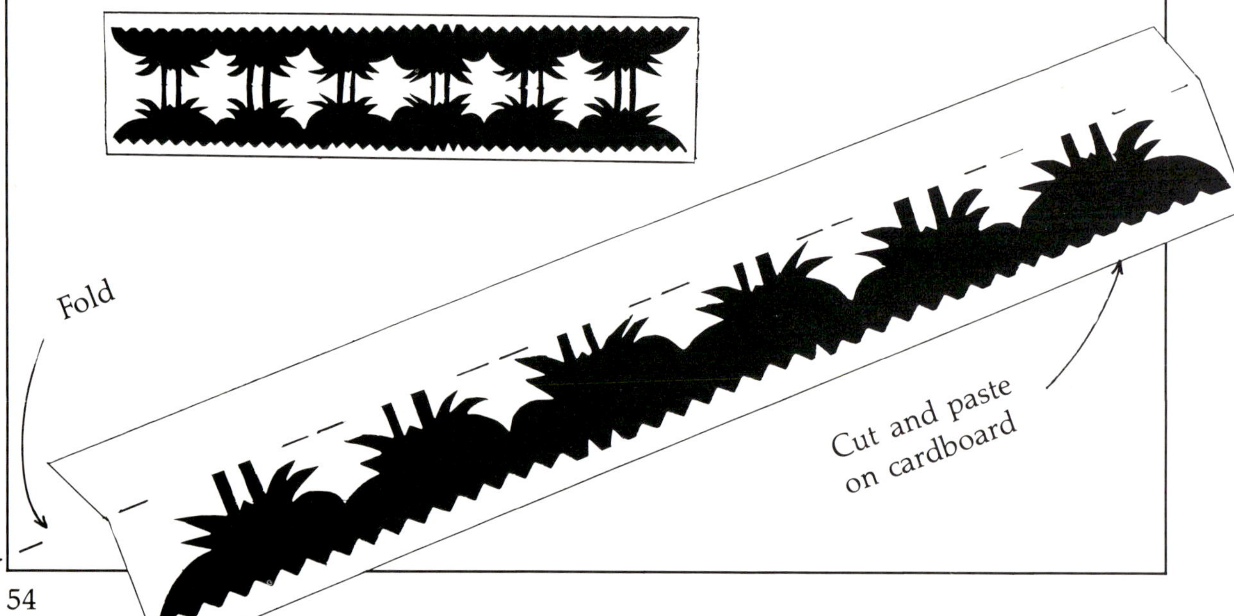

Have You Tasted *Kiełbasa?*

KIEŁBASA IS THE POLISH WORD for sausage. Polish sausage is very tasty. It has pork and lots of garlic in it. It is often served at Polish weddings and picnics. It used to be the custom for the men to make the sausage. The women made the cakes and other food.

People often travel long distances to go to a Polish wedding or picnic. Sometimes there are more than a thousand people. They always meet a lot of their friends from other towns there. They eat hundreds of pounds of sausage!

German Texans make lots of sausage too. They call it *wurst.* Today, Polish and German sausages are sold in stores all over the state of Texas.

. . . *Ogorki z Koprem?*

OGORKI Z KOPREM MEANS cucumbers with dill. They are Polish pickles. Polish pickles are large cucumbers which have been soaked in vinegar with garlic and dill. Polish-Texan families used to make huge jars of pickles. The children often came home from school and ate a pickle instead of a cookie. Some still do!

Look for Labels

Look for Polish pickles at the store. See if you can find a label that says OGoRKIz-KOPREM. There are more Polish words on the label. Can you figure them out?

Look around the store for more foods that have labels in other languages. Many of our foods come from other countries.

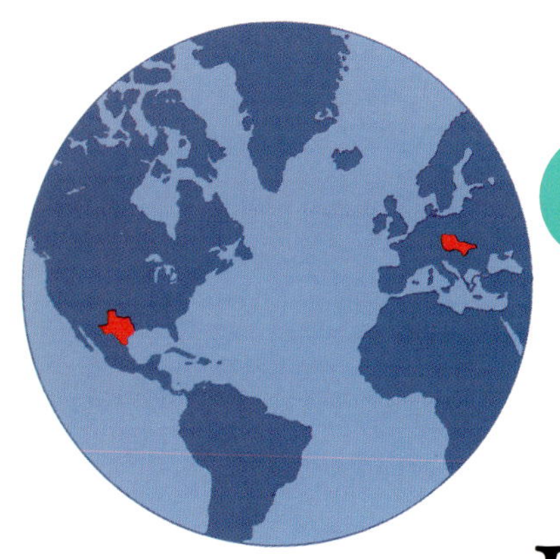

Czech Texans

IN 1852, 16 CZECH FAMILIES landed at Galveston. They were the first group of Czechs to arrive in Texas, although there were already a few Czech people in the state.

Most of the early Czech settlers were farmers. They settled in central Texas. Many lived in Fayette County.

The Czechs looked for good land for their farms. A story says that when they saw some good land, they turned off the road. They kept going until their ox carts got stuck in deep mud. This thick, black soil that stopped their carts would be good for growing crops, so that's where they settled.

Today, Czech Texans live all over the state. Many of them live and work in cities now. However, their grandfathers were probably farmers.

Life on a Farm

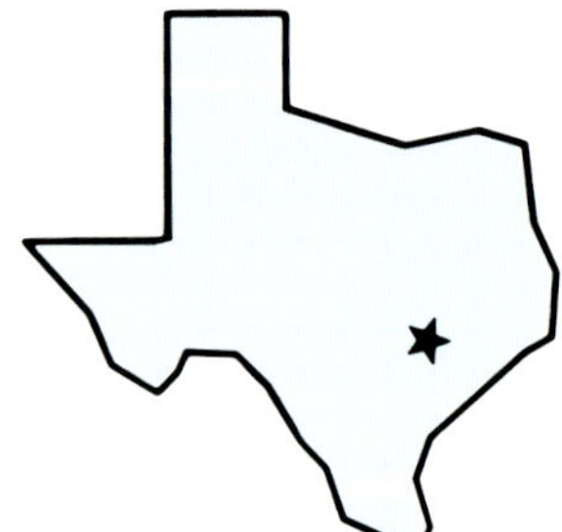

Fayetteville

HERE IS A STORY ABOUT a make-believe Czech family. A 10-year-old girl is talking. The time is 1900. The place is near Fayetteville.

"There are 12 people in our family. We live on a farm with a house and a barn. There are fields of cotton and corn and a vegetable garden near the house. We have some chickens and geese and a couple of cows. We have some pigs for meat and mules for plowing.

"Our whole family works in the fields. When the cotton is ready, we all pick it. We girls usually help Mother with the house and garden. We milk the cows too. The boys work mostly with Father. My brother Josef can pick 200 pounds of cotton in one day. That's hard work!"

Feather Stripping

"Sometimes we have to round up the geese for Mother. Jan grabs a goose and puts a sock over its head. Geese can nip! Then Mother holds the goose under her arm and plucks the feathers. It doesn't hurt the goose at all. She saves the feathers to put in a *perina,* a feather bed. It takes lots of feathers to make a *perina,* but it's nice and warm and cozy in winter!

"Some of the feathers have hard quills. We strip the soft part off the quills. We don't want quills in our *perina.* It is a big job to strip the feathers. Our fingers get sore. Sometimes Mother invites her friends to come and help.

"It's always fun when the neighbors come. They sing and tell stories while they work. Mother bakes dozens of *kolache,* the sweet rolls with a filling, to treat her helpers. It's like a party!"

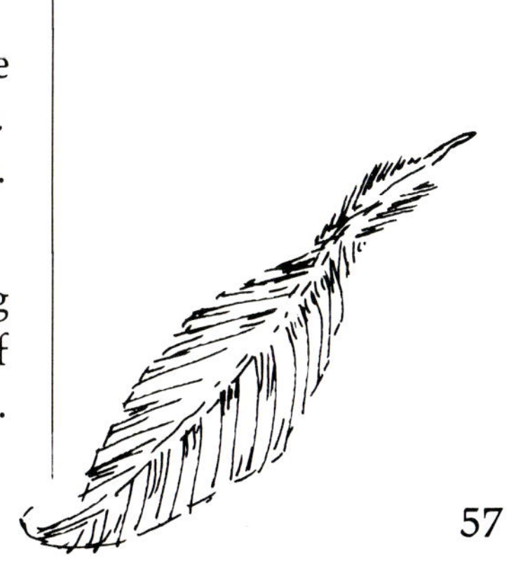

Homemade Egg Noodles

"On Sundays we like to eat chicken noodle soup. We all help make noodles, even Marie, who's three. Mother and I roll out the dough. We hang it over the backs of chairs to dry. Then we cut the noodles. The boys like to cut the noodles to see how thin they can make them. Sometimes they cut their fingers instead!"

Make Egg Noodles

Here is a recipe that Mrs. Annie Rozypal of Sinton wrote down for her friends.

Use as many egg yolks as you desire. For each egg yolk, measure ½ eggshell of water. Whip up egg and water. Add flour into mixture until it is impossible to get any more in. Now lay out on a floured board, and roll out as thin as possible (1/16 inch or less). Roll up and cut in strips. Lay out to dry. If desired, you may spread the whole sheet out over a line or chair back and let dry before cutting.

After you make the noodles, cook them in chicken broth. Then you will have chicken noodle soup like the Czech family made.

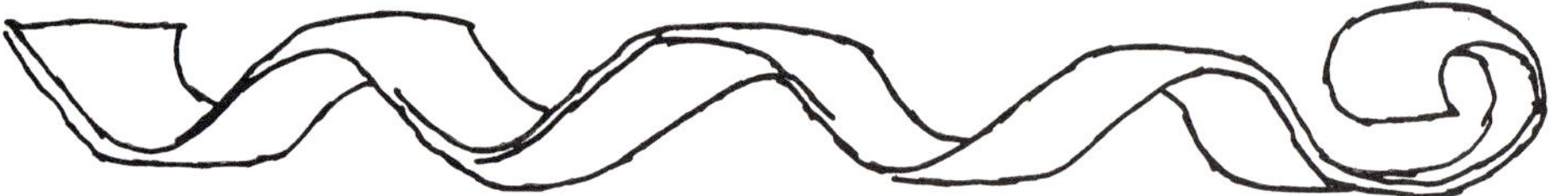

Play

"We don't just work. We play lots of games. The boys like to play *Na Kozla.* You get down on your hands and knees and make a line. The last one in line jumps over the rest until he gets to the front. Then the next person goes.

"At Easter, we decorate eggs. First we use goose quills to draw designs on the eggs with melted wax. Then we dye the eggs.

"We make most of our own toys. Sometimes we carve whistles out of twigs, and we make lots of things from paper, like snakes and fans and hats."

Cut Out a Snake

1. Cut out a paper circle 5 inches across.
2. Cut from the edge to the center in a spiral. The center becomes the head.
3. Stick the head on a pencil.
4. Move the pencil, and see the snake wiggle.

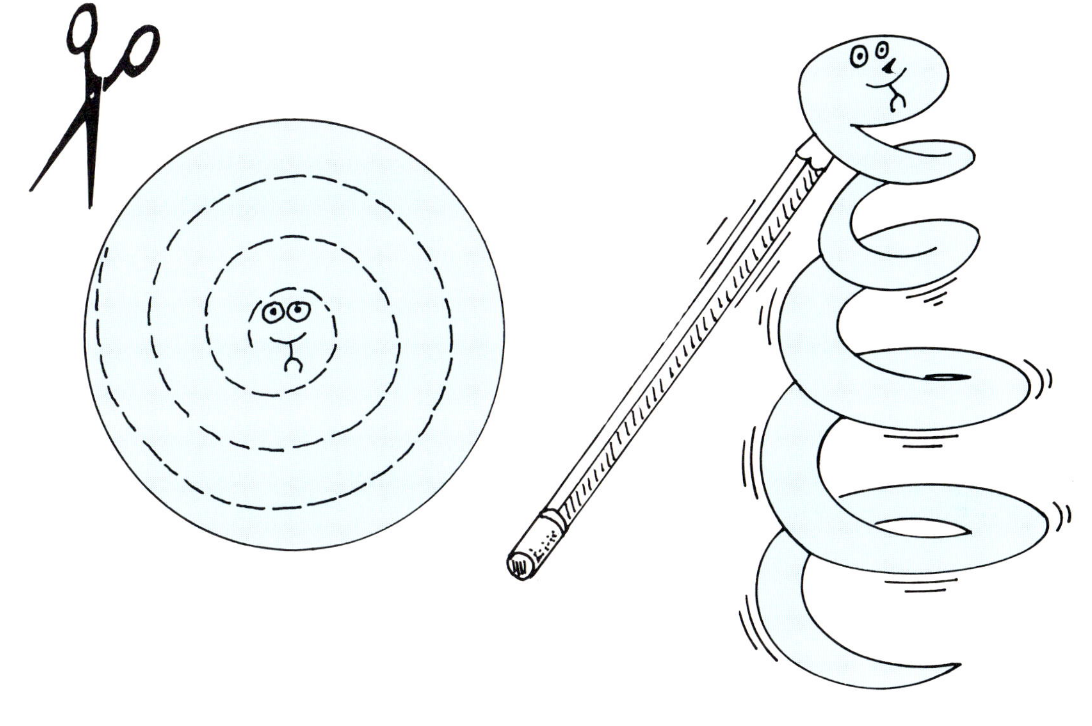

Family Customs

"There are some things we do, I don't know why. We run away from a cat if it is licking itself. If it looks at us first, that means we're going to get a whipping. When we lose a tooth, we throw it behind the stove. Then we ask a mouse to bring us a new one. I always grow another tooth, but I don't get whippings."

Music and Dance

"My father says *'Co Čech, to muzikant'*–'Every Czech is a musician.' It's true.

"Mother used to sing us to sleep with Czech songs, and we sing in church. Father carries a little folder with the words to songs in his pocket. Then we can sing together when we go visiting. The boys carry harmonicas in their pockets. They play them when we sing.

"Saturday nights are fun. We go visiting or to a dance. Czech bands play at the dances. The Baca Family Band has 13 brothers and sisters in it.

"We like to dance the polka. That's a Czech dance. It's fast and bouncy—you feel like you're galloping across the floor. Anna is only four, and she dances the polka with Mother. We dance so fast that we bump into each other!

"That's the way we live in our family. There are happy times; there are sad times. We work and we play; we sing and we dance. Our weddings last three days!"

The Czech Language

WHEN CZECHS CAME TO TEXAS, they wanted to keep their language. They started reading clubs, so that they could share books which were written in Czech. Many Czech newspapers were printed. These newspapers were sometimes used in Czech schools in Texas to help teach reading.

Today, many Texans speak Czech. It is the third language spoken in Texas, after English and Spanish.

Speak a Little Czech

Here is part of a Czech lesson from *Věstník*. *Věstník* is a Texas newspaper that is printed in both English and Czech.

Learn some of these words. How many of the words are like words in English? Use some of these words. Greet your friends in Czech.

Učme se Česky
Let Us Study Czech

Lekce Třeti— Lesson No. 3

Read the following exercises and words out LOUD with your parents or friends.

Jak se máte?— How are you?
Dobré ráno!— Good morning!
Na shledanou!— Good-bye! (Till we meet again.)

Slovníček— Vocabulary

matka— mother
hlava— head
dáma— lady
lampa— lamp
park— park
pán— gentleman
bratr— brother
čas— time
doktor (or lékař)— doctor
okno— window
škola— school
kočka— cat
ano— yes
co?— what?
ten, ta, to— that

Mluvnice— Grammar

1. Conjugation of the verb míti, "to

Learn Czech With Us

74th lesson. Revision Exercises

1) Form adjectives (-ivý, -ný, -cí, -tý, -avý, -telný):

dlouhotrvají- zima, lidé čekají- na autobus, benzín je hořl-, hra- hodiny, dobře uši- šaty, kvetou- stromy, bolest- rána, psa- stroj, vypra- prádlo, citl- mikrofon, auto stojí- před domem, krátce ostříha- vlasy, otevře- dveře, hlída- pes, pravd- příběh, koláč posypa- cukrem, nedopi- pivo, rozum- návrh, dobře uděla- práce, smrt- nemoc, kopa- míč, nevidi- síla, koupa- čepice

2) Form verbs (-it, -ovat, -at, et, -nout):

Auta park- na parkovišti. Lékař léč- nemocné. Chlapci se brzy skamarád-. Je pozdě, musíme spěch-. To pivo potřebuje *vy*chlad-. Eva umí dobře tanc-. Auto muselo náhle *za*brzd-. Musíte si to jídlo *při*sol-. Ten román se bude film-. Musíte více cvič-. Přednáška musí už každou chvíli skonč-. Je potřeba zmap- neznámé kraje. Musím si *vy*čist- boty. To slovo musím *vy*gum- (erase). Budeme závod-! Nejdříve musíme *vy*beton- základy domu. Beton (= concrete) musí dobře ztvrd-. Nemocný nesmí slad-. Pořád tomu nemůžu rozum-. Mužstvo muselo o vítězství boj-. Musím si

Sokols in Texas

*S*OKOL IS THE CZECH WORD FOR falcon, a bird that is strong and flies high. In Czechoslovakia, there used to be clubs called *sokols,* where people learned gymnastics and correct behavior. They made their bodies "strong and high-flying" by working out on bars and rings and other equipment. And they did exercises. Their motto was "a sound mind in a sound body."

Long ago, Czechs started *sokols* in Texas too. The first one met in a shed on a farm. A blacksmith nearby helped make the rings and the bars.

Today, there are several *sokols* in Texas. These are family clubs, where people of all ages can visit, dance, and learn gymnastics. They work out on equipment like bars and rings, and they tumble. Sometimes groups of girls wave colored ribbons in swoops and circles. You can try this too.

Make a Ribbon Wand

You will need:

a ribbon or crepe paper streamer 2 inches by 14 feet long

a wooden stick or rod ½ inch by 20 inches long

a metal screw eye

a string or thread 6 inches long

Use the screw eye and the string to fasten the ribbon to the stick (see picture). Make circles, figure 8's, and waves with your ribbon wand. Plan a group ribbon performance. Teams of athletes wave ribbon wands at the Olympic Games!

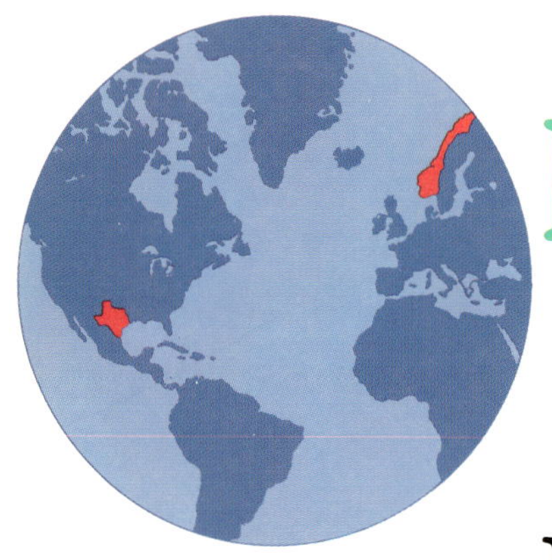

Norwegian Texans

IN 1854, A SMALL GROUP OF NORWEGIANS left east Texas to go to Bosque County. Bosque County was a new county in the middle of Texas. The state of Texas was giving away free land there. There were only a few people and not even a town in the whole county. However, the land was hilly, with meadows and forests and streams. It looked just like Norway.

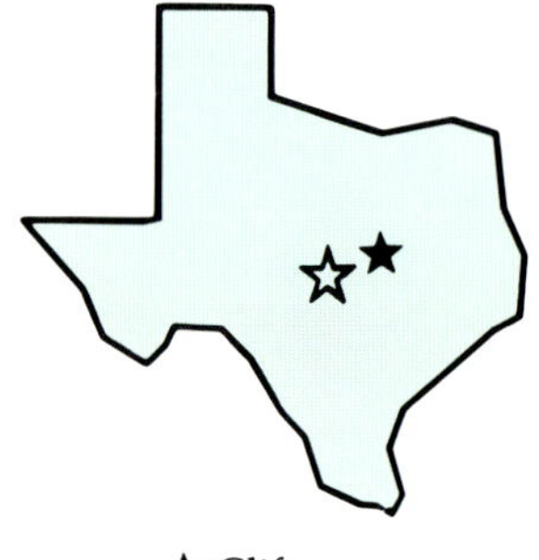

The Norwegians settled in the county and named their settlement Norse. Most of these people were farmers. They plowed the meadows and planted seeds. Their homes were several miles apart.

The first houses were built with logs from the forests. The roofs were steep. In Norway, houses were built with steep roofs, so that the snow would slide off. There wasn't much snow in Bosque County, but the Norwegians built houses with steep roofs anyway. That's what they were used to.

Later they built stone houses and a church. The church was at the center of their settlement. On Sundays, they spent all day at the church, so that they could worship and visit with each other.

More and more Norwegians came from other parts of Texas and from Norway to join their friends. In a few years, there were more Norwegians in Bosque County than anywhere else in Texas. Some began to live closer together in towns.

Today, descendants of these pioneers live in towns like Clifton and Cranfills Gap. Many grandparents remember life in Bosque County long ago.

Grandparents Tell Their Stories

MRS. MATTIE KNUDSON LIVES IN THE COUNTRY near Cranfills Gap. She is over 90 years old. She laughs a lot, and her hands are always busy. When friends come to see her, she serves coffee and cake – "Norwegians drink coffee morning, noon, and night."

Mrs. Knudson's grandparents came from Norway on a ship. Her grandmother brought her spinning wheel with her. They became farmers and also raised sheep.

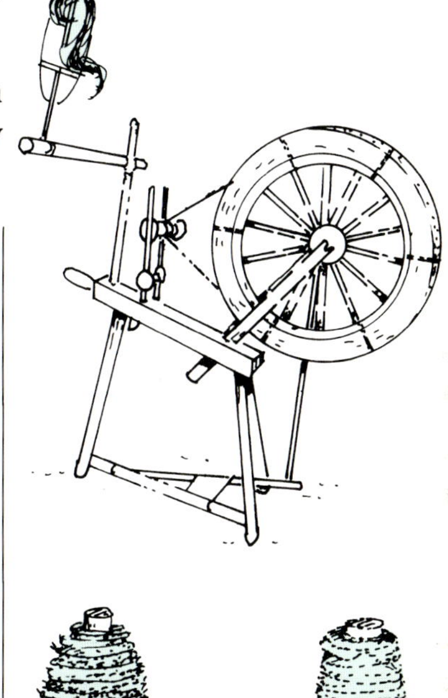

Her grandmother used her spinning wheel a lot. Mrs. Knudson said, "She spun wool from the sheep into yarn. She knitted stockings for us with the yarn. I didn't like those socks. They were black and ugly, and they were stickery. She knitted gloves out of the wool too. They went halfway up the fingers. My grandmother knitted all the time. She'd walk down the road to visit a neighbor, and she'd be knitting all the way.

"My mother doctored us when we had a bad cold. She heated two tablespoons of lard [pig fat] in a pan. Then she mixed in a tablespoon of coal oil, a teaspoon of turpentine, and a teaspoon of spirits of camphor. She put a piece of wool cloth in the mixture and laid the cloth on our chests. Sometimes we got well in 15 minutes."

Research Home Remedies

What does your mother give you for a sore throat? Do you sip lemon juice mixed with honey? What does she put on a bee sting? Does she use baking soda? These are home remedies.

Ask your grandmother how she took care of her family when they were sick. Ask other people too.

Another grandmother talked about her childhood.

"My mother died when I was five. My grandmother helped raise me. She told me about all the water in Norway. She said that they settled here because the land looked like Norway. There were forests, streams, and little mountains.

"She read me a comic strip called 'Ola and Per.' Ola and Per were two Norwegian Americans who did funny things. The comics were in a newspaper that came from Iowa. It was written in Norwegian.

En uheldig Flytning.
An Unfortunate Move

Why do you want to move the house up there, Per?
Polla says there is too little view at the bottom of the hill.
She thinks it's so beautiful to see the sun go down.

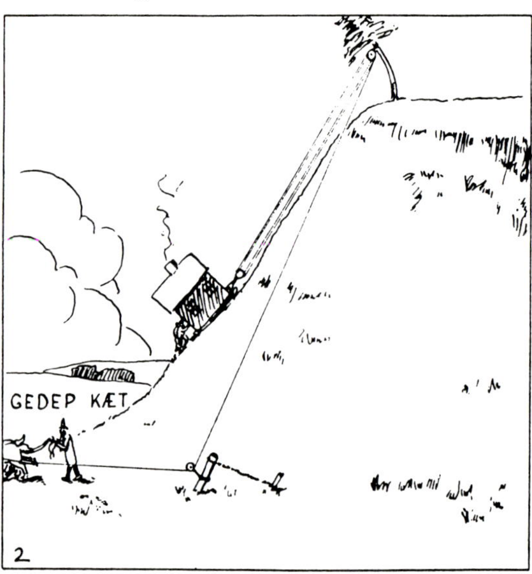

Giddy-ap!

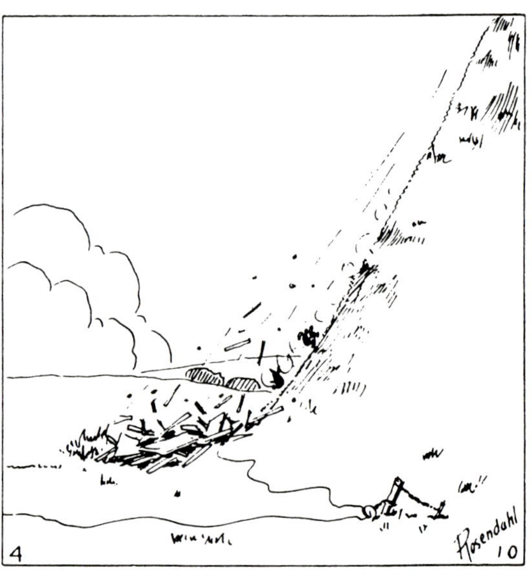

"We had *lutefisk*, or lye fish, and *flat brød*, flat bread, at Christmas time. Whenever we left the table, we'd have to say *'Takk for maten'* — 'Thank you for the food.' My grandmother would answer *'Vel be kommen'* — 'You're welcome.'

"When something went wrong, she'd say *'Uff da!'* — 'Oh my goodness!' Everyone said *'Uff da!'* They still do."

Mr. Lawrence Jenson said, "Every Norwegian family brought a Bible and a Lutheran hymnbook with them. When I was a boy, there was a Norwegian School every summer. It lasted for six weeks. We went to school all day. In the morning, we studied the Bible. In the afternoon, we learned to read and write Norwegian. We already spoke it."

Mr. John Homerstad played a game like "Ride a Cockhorse" with his grandmother.

"My grandmother used to dance me on her knee. She'd say —

'Ride, ride ranke	**'Ride, ride [on the knee].**
Hesten heter Blanke,	**The horse is called Bright One.**
Nei, men det er ikke så,	**No, but that is not so,**
For han heter epelgrå.	**For he is dapple-gray.**
Tre små dukker spiste kake,	**Three small dolls are eating cake**
Tre små hunder satt på bordet	**And three small dogs are sitting on the table**
Sa vov-vov-vov.	**Saying 'Bow-wow-wow!' "**

Remember a Family Rhyme

Did your grandparents or parents play rhyme games with you? Did they tell you rhymes? Remember a family rhyme. Ask where it came from.

Mr. Homerstad also talked about *Jule-bukking,* an old Norwegian custom.

"Our Christmas started on Christmas Eve and lasted for 13 days. After Christmas Day, we went *Jule-bukking.* We visited the neighbors and wore masks, so they wouldn't know who we were.

"First, we'd dress up in old clothes, like an old man's costume, and put on a mask. Some of us made masks from flour sacks. We'd cut out the mouth and eyes, and paint the face with paint. Some kids made their masks out of paper bags. Then we'd get together in a group. Sometimes there would be 15 or 20 of us.

"We'd knock on the door and walk in. No one locked their doors then. The people would say 'Who in the world is that? I'm so scared! Did a stranger come in?' After they guessed who we were, they would give us hot chocolate and cookies. Sometimes we'd go *Jule-bukking* for several nights."

Today in Bosque County

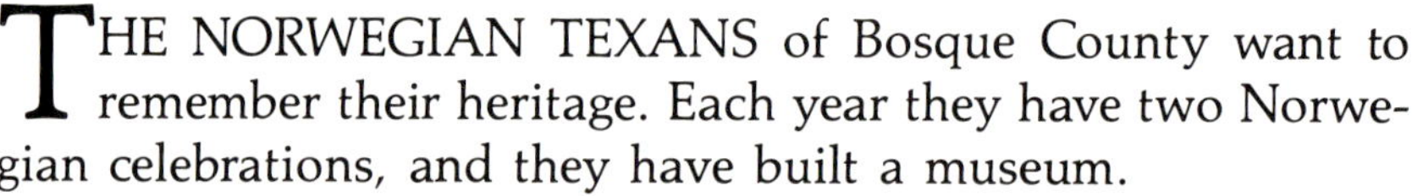

THE NORWEGIAN TEXANS of Bosque County want to remember their heritage. Each year they have two Norwegian celebrations, and they have built a museum.

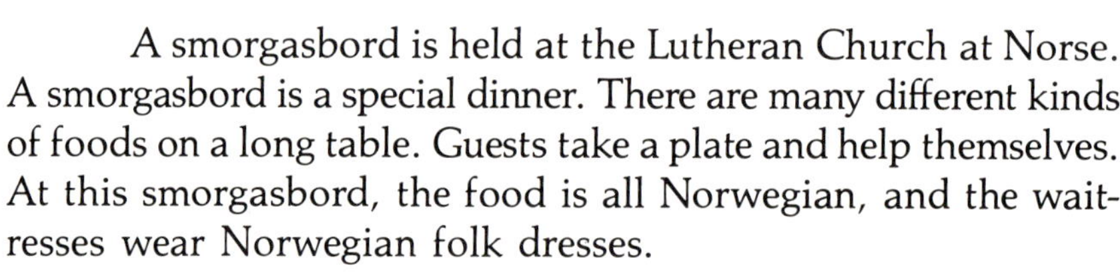

A smorgasbord is held at the Lutheran Church at Norse. A smorgasbord is a special dinner. There are many different kinds of foods on a long table. Guests take a plate and help themselves. At this smorgasbord, the food is all Norwegian, and the waitresses wear Norwegian folk dresses.

In December, there is a *lutefisk* dinner at the high school in Cranfills Gap. *Lutefisk* was a favorite food in Norway. It was also served on Christmas Eve. Norwegian Texans could not get this food very often, so they served it just at Christmastime.

Lutefisk is dried codfish. It is soaked for three days in lye water and for three days in lime water. Then it is soaked for four days in clear water before it is cooked. For the dinner in Cranfills Gap, more than 400 pounds of fish are ordered from Norway. The fish comes in large pieces that look like gray boards. After it is soaked, there are over 1,000 pounds of thick, juicy, white fish.

Lutefisk is served with boiled potatoes, melted butter, and white sauce. Have you ever eaten an all-white dinner? Some Norwegian Texans love to eat *lutefisk* for Christmas. Others eat turkey instead.

The museum in Clifton contains many objects that Norwegian Texans used long ago. There are painted chests, looms, spinning wheels, and mangle boards. In the early days the women wove woolen yarn into material to make clothes. They used the mangle boards to press the clothes before they had irons. Today, many people can learn about the early settlers from these objects which have been saved and collected.

Make a Museum

Do you have objects at your house that your grandparents or great-grandparents used? Perhaps there is an old iron or a quilt or a grinder. Collect some interesting things. Write facts about them on cards, and make a display. You can learn about family history this way.

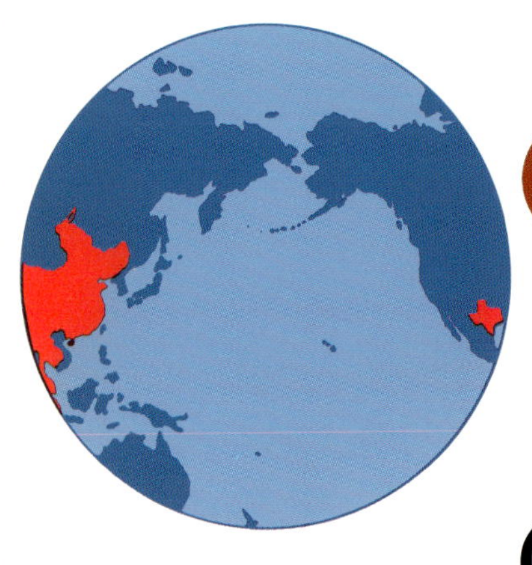

Chinese Texans

GROUPS OF CHINESE MEN came to Texas more than 100 years ago. They came to help build the railroads across the state. Hearne, Toyah, and El Paso were some of the towns where they settled.

Between 1882 and 1943, the U.S. government did not allow many Chinese people to enter the United States. However, in 1917, about 500 Chinese people were allowed to settle in San Antonio. These people had been living in Mexico. When an expedition of American soldiers went to Mexico, the Chinese gave them food and supplies. When the Americans left Mexico, the Chinese followed them. They were permitted to enter the U.S. because they had helped the soldiers.

Since 1943, many more Chinese people have come to Texas. They live mostly in cities. Houston has more Chinese Texans than any other city in Texas. There are shopping centers with signs in Chinese. A Chinese-language newspaper is printed there. Chinese is spoken in Chinese theaters and churches. And there is always a Dragon Parade in the streets on the Lunar New Year.

The Lunar New Year

MANY CHINESE-TEXAN FAMILIES celebrate the Lunar New Year. This holiday comes after the New Year that is celebrated on January 1st. Long ago, in China, each month began with the new moon. This caused the New Year to come in late January or February. Each year was named after an animal.

The Lunar New Year is a family celebration with dinners and gifts. Also, ancestors are honored with food and prayers.

It is important to have a clean home and to not owe any money to start the new year. Families clean house and wash all the clothes and sheets. They cook for many days to get ready. On New Year's Day, it is bad luck to have a speck of dust in the house or to cook any food. No one is even supposed to take out the trash or to sweep. Sweeping will sweep good fortune out of the house. Also, no one is supposed to say any bad words, tell a lie, or break a dish. If anyone does, bad luck will follow that person into the new year.

On New Year's Eve, there is a big family dinner. Everyone wears new clothes. The children get up early on New Year's morning and greet their parents. Sometimes they bow and say "I wish you prosperity" in Chinese. Then the children receive red envelopes with money inside. Red is the color for good luck and happiness. The bills or coins are in even numbers. Odd numbers are bad luck.

On New Year's Day, people visit their relatives and friends. They share a holiday meal. There is always chicken, pork, beef, and fish. The chicken and fish are served with their heads and tails on. This means the beginning and the end. And there is also *fung chung,* a red Chinese sausage, for good luck.

Houston has dragon parades. Men walk through the streets carrying a long papier-mâché and cloth dragon over their heads. This dragon, called King Lung, has been a part of Chinese celebrations for hundreds of years. In other cities, there are sometimes dragon dances, so people won't forget the Chinese customs.

Celebrate a Chinese New Year

Make a red envelope, like the one pictured on this page. Put two pennies in it. Give it to a friend and say "I wish you prosperity."

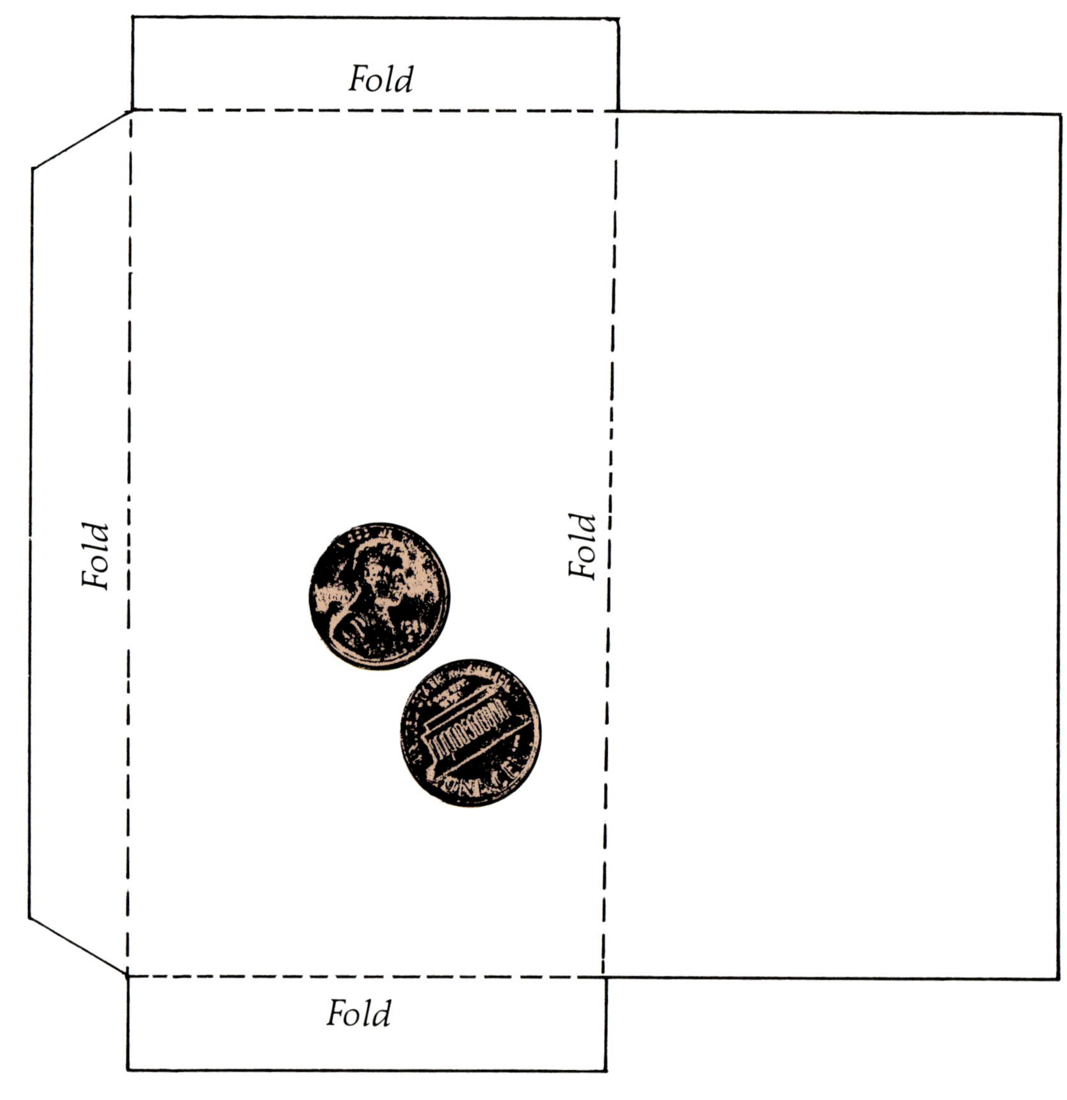

Firecrackers and New Year's

Did you know that firecrackers were invented in China? Firecrackers are an important part of the Lunar New Year celebration in China. The Wong family of San Antonio used to buy dozens and dozens of firecrackers and rockets each year. They exploded them on January 1st, like their neighbors did. However, they really were observing the Chinese New Year custom. Mrs. Virginia Wong said,

> "We hung strings of them on clothes hangers on the front porch, and we hung rockets from the trees. We used to set off strings of firecrackers in front of the door to keep evil spirits away. The old story is that evil spirits walk the earth looking for a nice home to go into. They decide that a house with exploding firecrackers is an awful place, and they go next door instead. There were always firecrackers left over. We exploded them on the 4th of July."

The Wongs like having two New Year's celebrations. They make New Year's resolutions both times.

Mrs. Wong said, "Now we go to our grandparents' to celebrate the Lunar New Year, because the old people enjoy keeping all the customs."

How the Years Were Named

ESTHER WU GREW UP IN San Antonio. Her grandmother, who lived with the family, told Esther many stories. Here is a story she told about a New Year's party in China long ago.

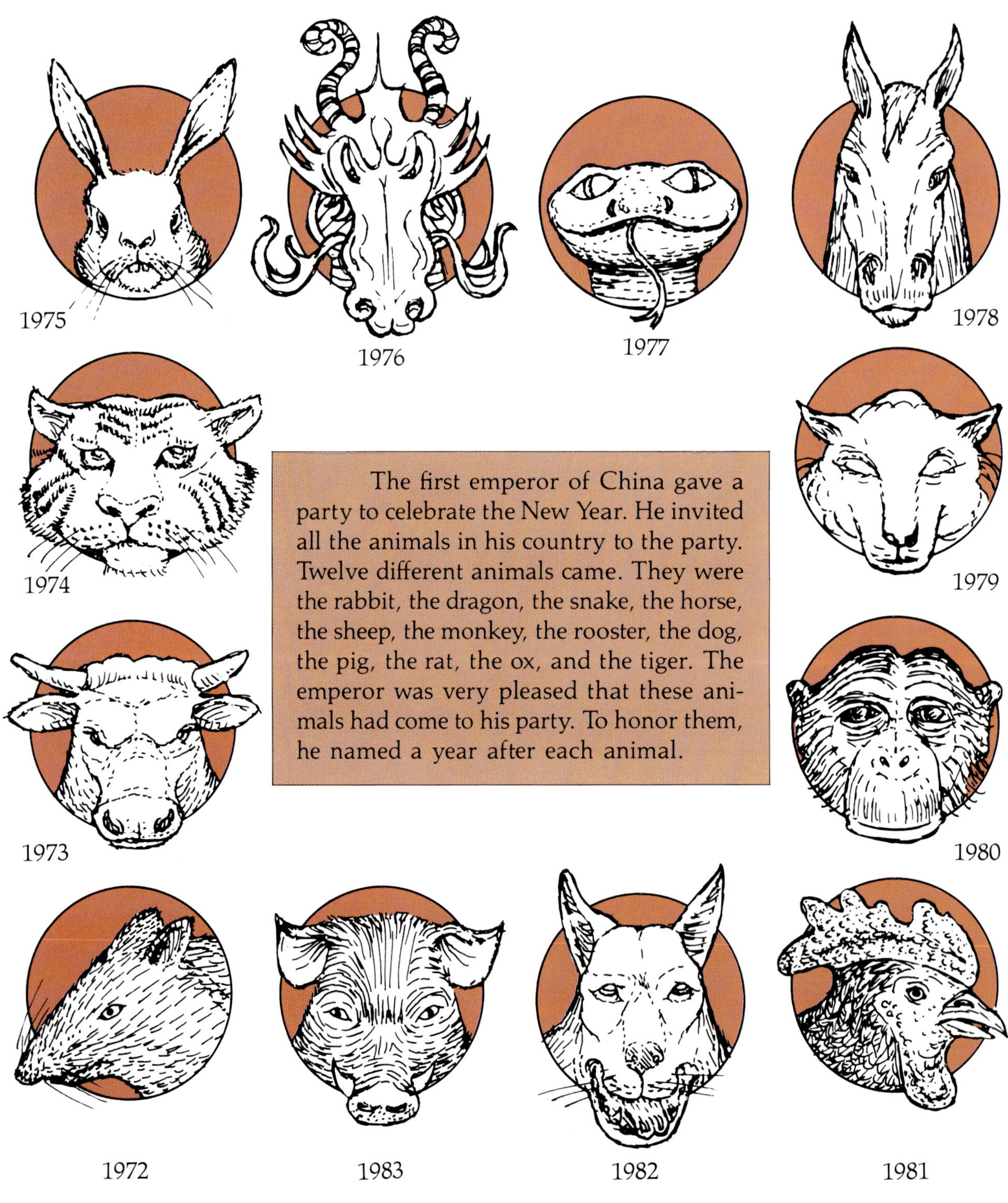

The first emperor of China gave a party to celebrate the New Year. He invited all the animals in his country to the party. Twelve different animals came. They were the rabbit, the dragon, the snake, the horse, the sheep, the monkey, the rooster, the dog, the pig, the rat, the ox, and the tiger. The emperor was very pleased that these animals had come to his party. To honor them, he named a year after each animal.

Chinese people feel that the year of their birth is special. Esther was born in the Year of the Dragon. Which Chinese year were you born in?

Calculate Chinese Years

Was your mother born in the Year of the Dragon? Let's find out.

Write down the year in which she was born. Keep adding 12 to that number until the year matches one on the page to the left. What animal appears above that year? Is it a dragon?

You can calculate Chinese birth years for other members of your family too.

Chinese Schools in Texas

THERE ARE SEVERAL CHINESE SCHOOLS in Texas. The oldest one is in San Antonio. The Chinese School at the Chinese Community Cultural Center in Houston has more than 300 students. The children are from 4 to 16 years old. They go to their regular school five days a week and then take classes at the Chinese School on Saturday or Sunday. They study the Chinese language. There are also classes in arts and crafts, drama, dance, and kung fu. Many boys like to study kung fu and often come early to practice. Some girls take the kung fu class too.

The Chinese Language

THE CHINESE LANGUAGE IS very different from English. It is written in characters, which are like pictures. Each character stands for a different word. Students have to memorize hundreds and hundreds of characters.

Copy Chinese Characters

Here are some Chinese characters. Notice the characters for "sit," "forest," and "bright." What other characters were combined to form them?

Copy some of these characters. Many Chinese people use a brush and black ink to paint the characters. They are very beautiful.

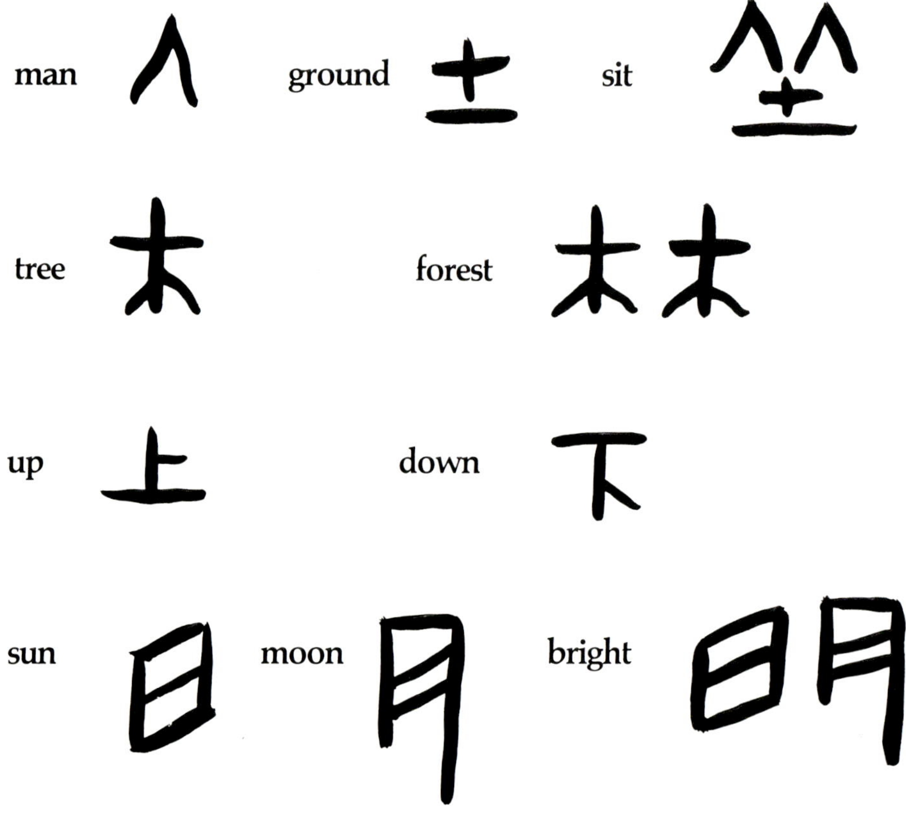

Chinese-Texan Food

ALTHOUGH CHINESE TEXANS EAT THE SAME kinds of food as other Texans, they often have Chinese foods. When they eat these foods, they sometimes eat with chopsticks. Rice is served at every meal. The older people drink hot tea in small cups without handles. The children like iced tea or soft drinks.

The food is cooked in a *wok,* a pan with a rounded bottom. Meat and vegetables are cut into small pieces and cooked quickly in a little oil. This kind of cooking is called stir-frying.

Many families have gardens and grow their own Chinese vegetables, such as winter melon and long green beans. Some of these beans are 20 inches long! Many families serve a soup made of winter melon. This soup is a kind of health food. It helps the body to digest a meal. Chinese Texans serve this soup often.

Many restaurants in Texas serve Chinese food. Egg rolls, sweet and sour pork, and *wonton* soup are some favorite dishes. Children also like Chinese fortune cookies.

Visit a Chinese Restaurant

Taste some Chinese food. Try eating with chopsticks. Study the menu. Look at how the restaurant is decorated. Notice the colors, the dishes, the pictures, the lights.

What can you learn in a Chinese restaurant?

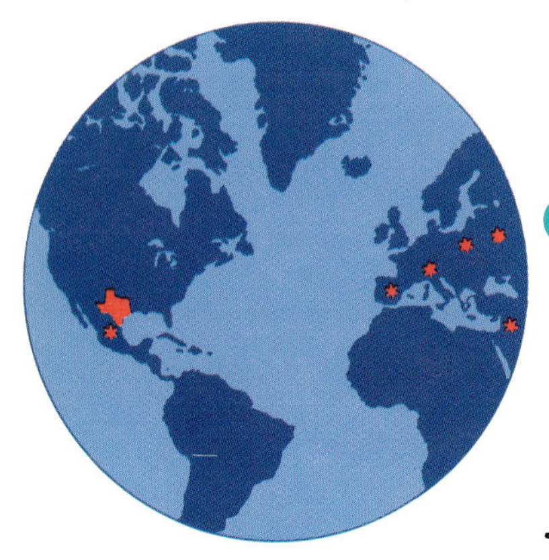

Jewish Texans

JEWISH TEXANS CAME FROM many countries, not just one. Most came from Germany and eastern European countries such as Russia, Poland, Lithuania, and Austria-Hungary. A few came from countries like Spain, Mexico, and Syria. They all spoke different languages.

Although they came from different places, the Jewish people are alike in many ways. They share a history and religion passed down from an ancient group of people who lived in Canaan, now Israel. Their Bible is written in Hebrew, a language of those people.

Almost 2,000 years ago, the Jews had to leave their homeland. They settled in many different parts of the world. They took their customs with them. In some countries they were not allowed to practice their religion. Many Jews who wished to keep their Jewish customs and traditions came to Texas.

Make a Star of David

The Star of David is the symbol for the Jewish religion. It is a six-pointed star.

1. Cut six strips of paper ¼ inch by 4 inches (or you can use popsicle sticks).
2. Fasten three strips of paper (or sticks) together to make a triangle. Make two triangles.

3. Lay one triangle on top of the other, and turn it until there are six points.
4. Glue the triangles together to make a six-pointed star.

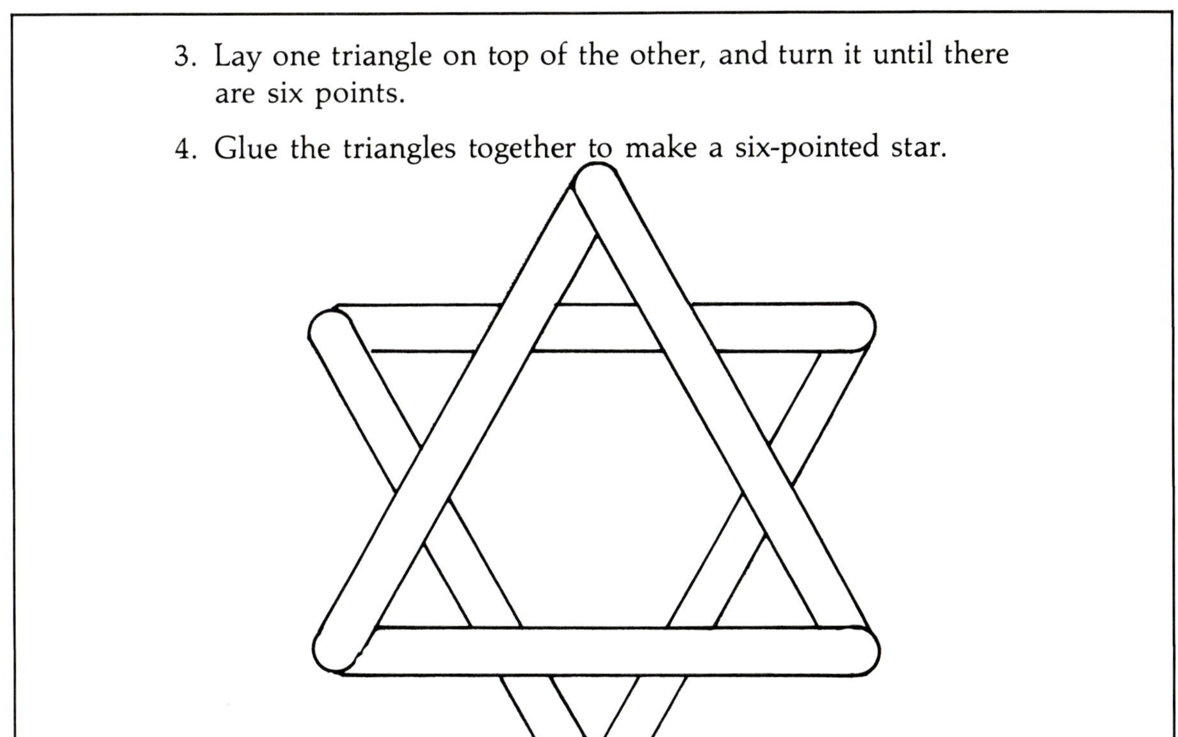

The Rabbi from Galveston

IN 1888, HENRY COHEN ARRIVED in Galveston. He had grown up in England and had become a rabbi. A rabbi is a Jewish teacher and minister. He came to serve at the synagogue, a Jewish place of worship.

Rabbi Cohen came to Galveston with 1,000 books and a stutter. When he gave his first sermon, one of the young ladies giggled because he stuttered. Not everyone minded his stutter. He was a fine teacher, and they liked what he said.

The rabbi practiced his sermons by talking with pebbles in his mouth. He practiced on the beach, where no one could hear him. After a while, he was able to speak without a stutter. And the young lady who had giggled became his wife. Rabbi Cohen and "Miss Molly" were married in a Jewish wedding.

Rabbi Cohen traveled a great deal in his work. There weren't many Jewish people in Texas then, and they were widely scattered. When the rabbi came to Texas, there were only seven synagogues in the whole state. The people in small towns didn't have a synagogue or a rabbi. Every week Rabbi Cohen traveled to towns as far away as Brownsville and Nacogdoches. He married people, and he held funerals. He taught classes and held religious services.

The Galveston Movement

In 1907, Rabbi Cohen offered to help Jewish immigrants who came to Galveston. Jews in eastern Europe were not allowed to practice their religion, and many were even killed. A large number of Jews wanted to escape to America. Most of them went to New York City. There was not enough work for them there, and they lived in very crowded rooms. Jewish leaders in New York decided to send Jewish immigrants to other cities instead.

Their plan was to send the Jewish immigrants to Galveston first. Ships from Europe often landed in Galveston. Also, there were railroads from Galveston to many western cities. People who could make shoes or cut meat or build houses were needed in these cities. There would be jobs for the immigrants in the West. Rabbi Cohen and others helped the immigrants when they arrived in Galveston.

The Landing of the Cassel

The steamship *Cassel* arrived in Galveston with 87 Jewish immigrants on board. They had traveled in a crowded area below the deck. They were tired, dirty, hungry, and afraid.

Rabbi Cohen and others welcomed the immigrants and took them to their offices. The immigrants bathed at last, to clean up after the long journey. They were given food and clothing.

Soon the mayor of Galveston came to meet them. He shook their hands and offered to help them. They could hardly believe their ears. They were not used to such kindness.

A Job for Everyone

Finally the immigrants boarded trains to go to their new homes. A butcher went to Fort Worth. A carpenter went to Kansas City. Each man was sent to a city where he was needed.

For several years, Rabbi Cohen met every boat. Over 10,000 immigrants were given jobs in western cities. Today, many Texans have grandparents who were helped by Rabbi Cohen and the Jewish Immigrants' Information Bureau.

The Jewish Home

MANY JEWISH FAMILIES FASTEN a *mezuzah* on the doorpost of their front door. This is a little box with a scroll inside. Verses from the Bible are written on the scroll. A *mezuzah* on the doorpost means that the house is a Jewish home.

The home is the center of the Jewish community. Long ago, Jews in many countries were not allowed to build synagogues. They met in their homes to worship. Today, there are lots of synagogues in Texas, but Jews still worship in their homes too.

The Sabbath

THE MOST IMPORTANT HOLIDAY for the Jews is on the seventh day of each week. It is called the Sabbath. The Sabbath begins Friday at sundown and ends on Saturday at sundown. On Friday evening, many Jewish families gather at the Sabbath table in their home. On the table are candles, a cup of wine, and a braided loaf of bread called *hallah*. First the candles are lighted, usually by the mother. Then a parent, usually the father, says prayers over the wine and the bread. Everyone takes sips of the wine and breaks the bread. Afterwards, they eat supper.

Rebecca told about her family's Sabbath in San Antonio. "We light two candles at our house. Mother bakes our *hallah*. We call it 'cloud bread' because it puffs up all over like a cloud."

After supper, the family often goes to the synagogue. People greet each other, saying *"Shabbat shalom"* — "Peace on the Sabbath." The Sabbath is a day of rest and quiet. Some Jews do not even drive their cars or cook on the Sabbath.

How do you or your Jewish friends observe the Sabbath?

Hebrew School

MANY JEWISH CHILDREN ATTEND Hebrew School. Classes are usually held at the synagogue in the late afternoons. The children learn to read Hebrew, and they study about their religion.

Rebecca attends Hebrew School. She is learning to read Hebrew. She said, "We have an English name and a Hebrew name. My name in Hebrew sounds like 'Rivka.' It looks like this in print — רִבְקָה . It looks like this in cursive — רִבְקָה ."

From a lesson in Rebecca's book

Name These Objects

Here are some objects that have special meaning for Jewish Texans. See if you can match the pictures with the descriptions.

The Torah is part of the Bible. It is written in Hebrew on a scroll. Every synagogue has a Torah.

A *shofar* is a musical instrument, which is made from a ram's horn. It is one of the oldest instruments in the world. It makes a loud, shrill sound. The *shofar* is blown during the Jewish New Year, which comes in September or October.

A *menorah* is a candleholder. This *menorah* is used at Hanukkah, a holiday that comes in late November or December. Hanukkah lasts for eight days. Each evening, the family lights a new candle, until all eight candles are burning.

A *yarmulke* is a skullcap. Many Jewish men and boys wear a *yarmulke* when they pray or study about their religion. Some Jews wear a *yarmulke* all the time.

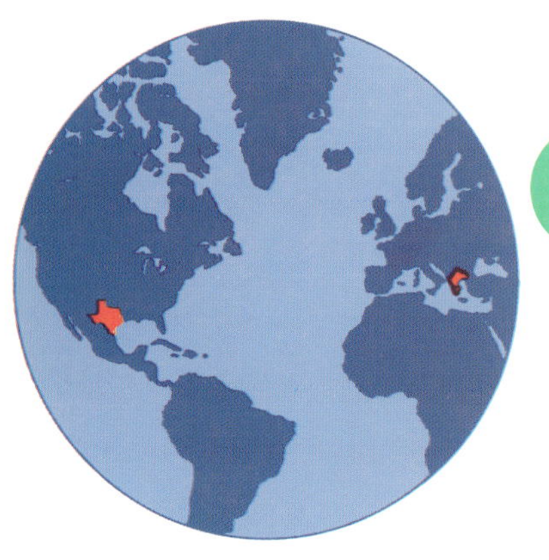

Greek Texans

A HUNDRED YEARS AGO, there was a small Greek community in Galveston. Some of the Greeks were fishermen and sailors who had come from Greece to the Texas coast. Others worked in restaurants or stores. Some became owners of businesses. Most Greeks who came to Texas long ago lived in cities like Houston, Fort Worth, Dallas, and San Antonio.

Two Greek-Texan Children

SPIRO AND MARY LIVE IN San Antonio. Spiro is in the seventh grade, and Mary is in the fourth grade. They both like sports and Greek dancing. They attend the Greek Orthodox Church. Their grandparents came from Greece, and Spiro and Mary are proud of their Greek heritage.

The Church

The church is a very important part of Greek life. Every Sunday, Spiro and Mary attend St. Sophia Greek Orthodox Church. They can smell the incense before they open the door. The back of the church is dark. Their grandmother lights a tall, thin candle. After Sunday school downstairs, Spiro and Mary join the older people in church. The priest sings the words of the service in Greek and in English.

Greek School

Every Monday afternoon from four to five o'clock, Mary and Spiro go to Greek School at the church. They are learning to read and write Greek. They speak a little Greek in their home, mostly with their grandmother.

At school, they write their names in Greek in the roll book. Their names look like this—

Mary or Maria- Μαρία

Spiro – Σπίρος

Greek Treats

Mary and Spiro like Greek food. They eat it at church dinners and festivals. The women from their church enjoy getting together to cook Greek food for special occasions. They cook for days and days sometimes! Mary and Spiro's mother often cooks Greek food at home too. They really like her pastries and chicken soup!

Discover Greek Foods

Here are some Greek foods that Mary and Spiro like. See if you can match the words and pictures.

1. *Dolmathes* are made of rice and meat wrapped in grape leaves.
2. *Feta* cheese is white and is made from goat's milk.
3. Olive oil is used in salads and many other Greek dishes.
4. *Baklava* is a pastry with many thin layers of *phyllo* (dough) and nuts. It melts in your mouth.

St. Basil's Cake

On New Year's Day, Spiro and Mary look forward to cutting the *vasilopita,* or St. Basil's Cake. The cake always has a lucky coin baked inside. The children's aunt told them the story of how this custom began.

In ancient times, a Greek city was captured by barbarians. The barbarians said that they would not kill the people if they gave them their money and jewels. A leader in the city, St. Basil, collected all the riches, so that the people could be saved. Then a strange thing happened. The barbarians became sick, and many died. The rest of them left the city without taking anything.

St. Basil wanted to return the riches, but he didn't know who owned them. He asked all the bakers to bake cakes with the coins and jewels in them. Then he gave the cakes to the people in the city, and everyone shared the riches.

Since then, on January 1st, Greek Orthodox families have served a special cake with a coin in it. January 1st is St. Basil's feast day. When the cake is cut, the person who finds the coin expects to have good luck during the new year.

Mary and Spiro's mother puts a dime wrapped in waxed paper in her cake. Mary said, "I didn't get the coin this year. Last year I got one and kept it, and I had good luck all year."

The Blessing of the Waters

THE BLESSING OF THE WATERS is a religious custom. Greek Orthodox people all over the world celebrate this custom. It takes place on or near January 6th.

The Blessing of the Waters took place in Corpus Christi recently. Some people from St. Sophia Church in San Antonio drove there for the ceremony.

A priest stood on a platform by the Gulf of Mexico. He released a dove into the air. Then he blessed the waters and asked God to keep those on the sea and in the waters safe. Eight boys stood in the cold water. The priest threw a wooden cross high over their heads out into the gulf, and the boys went after it. The boy who brought back the cross received a special blessing from the priest.

Spiro is a swimmer. He would like to take part in the Blessing of the Waters when he is older. His mother hopes that he will bring back the cross some day.

1985

1986

Easter and Red Eggs

EASTER IS THE MOST IMPORTANT holiday of the year for Spiro and Mary. The Greek Orthodox Easter is usually later than Easter in other churches.

At midnight before Easter Day, people gather in the church. Everyone has a candle. During the service, the priest turns off the lights, so the church is in darkness. Then he lights one candle. The flame is passed from person to person until the church is filled with light. The people leave the church with lighted candles and bright red eggs. The red eggs mean "new life."

Easter Day is a big celebration with family dinners or picnics. There is often a bowl of red hard-cooked eggs on the table. Greek people play an Easter game with the eggs. It's good luck to win. Spiro and Mary play this game every year. It wouldn't be Easter without it!

Play the Easter Egg Game

Any number of people can play this game. All you need are hard-cooked eggs. Hold an egg in your fingers. Bump the end of your egg against the end of another person's egg. If your egg cracks, you are out. If your egg remains whole, bump eggs with someone else. The last person without a cracked egg is the winner.

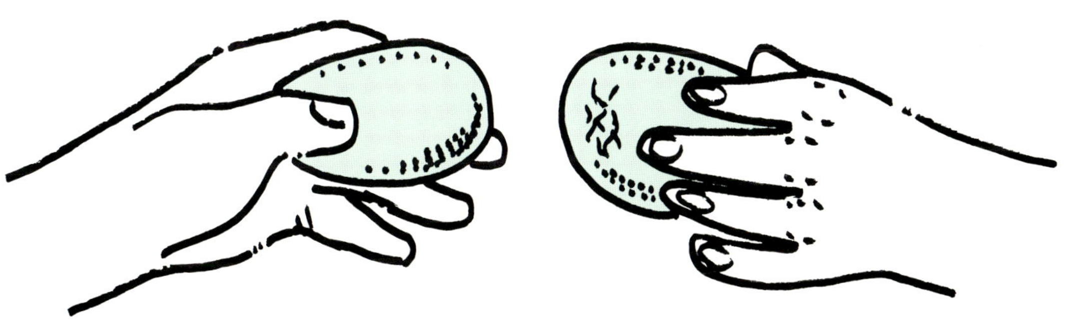

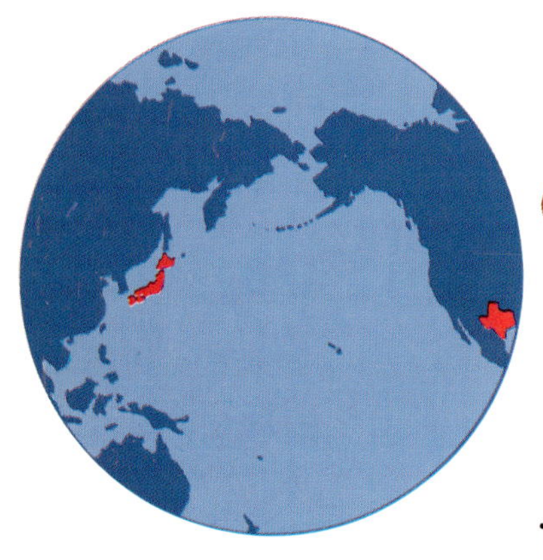

Japanese Texans

LONG AGO, THERE WERE ONLY A FEW Japanese people in Texas. Some early pioneer families settled near Houston and Beaumont. Other Japanese families came to the lower Rio Grande Valley. Most of these people were farmers. They grew rice, mandarin oranges, cantaloupes, soybeans, and many other crops. Some of them grew flowers, shrubs, and trees for homes and gardens.

Today, many people travel between Texas and Japan. Japanese people are building factories and opening businesses in Texas. There are many more Japanese Texans now.

A Japanese-Texan Pioneer

IN 1903, SEITO SAIBARA CAME TO Texas to look at the country near Houston. He wanted to buy some land on which to grow rice. Rice was, and still is, the main food in Japan. Mr. Saibara dreamed of starting a colony of Japanese rice farmers in Texas.

Here are some lines from Mr. Saibara's pocket diary. He wrote in his diary almost every day.

[August] 25th
Got up at 6 a.m. and was looking at . . . fields from the train. At 10 a.m. arrived at Houston. . . .

[September] 14th
Saw the land in Webster [near Houston]. . . .

October 9th
. . . I promised to buy 304 acres. . . .

23rd
Moved to Webster. This day the weather is fine and I felt magnificent.

24th
. . . Plowed . . . and sowed *negi, shungiku, mana, hojona,* etc. [vegetables eaten in Japan].

November 3rd
Since today is the Emperor's birthday, rested all afternoon.

After he was settled on his land, Mr. Saibara sent for his family and friends. They arrived in January 1904.

Growing Rice

Mr. Saibara and his son planted rice in the spring. His wife had brought the seeds from Japan. Then they flooded the fields with water. The rice plants grew in the water. When the rice grains were ripe, the Saibaras drained the water off the fields and harvested the rice. It was a good crop. The rice was sold as seeds for other Texas farmers to plant.

The Saibara rice fields became known all over the world. People came from many places to visit them. Now these rice lands have been sold. The Lyndon B. Johnson Space Center has been built on a piece of that land.

Rice has become an important crop in Texas partly because of Japanese rice farmers.

A Mystery!

IN THE 1930's, THE JAPANESE TEXANS in the Rio Grande Valley put together a magazine. They called it *Hana Kago,* or *Flower Basket.* It contained stories and poems which they had composed. The magazine was written in Japanese and printed once a month.

In the 1940's, Japan and the United States were at war. People from the U.S. Government searched the homes of Japanese Americans. They took away materials that were written in Japanese. Many Japanese Texans destroyed papers and magazines that were written in Japanese, so that they wouldn't get into trouble.

Today, not a single copy of *Hana Kago* can be found. Wouldn't it be exciting if someone could discover a copy? Perhaps there is one hidden behind a wall. Perhaps someone mailed a magazine to a relative in Japan. Could there be one in some U.S. Government office?

There must be a copy somewhere! This is a real mystery! Maybe a student in Texas or Japan can solve it.

Haiku

A *HAIKU* IS A SHORT POEM INVENTED by the Japanese. Many women and men in Japan, even government leaders, write this kind of poetry. Here is a famous Japanese *haiku* by Bashō. The people who wrote poems for *Hana Kago* probably knew it by heart.

Furu-ike ya	**An old pond—**
kawazu tobi-komu	**A frog jumps in—**
mizu-no-oto.	**Splash!**

Look at this poem. The Japanese *haiku* is about something in nature. There are three lines. The first line has five syllables, the second has seven syllables, and the third has five syllables. The lines do not rhyme.

Here is a *haiku* written by some Texas fifth graders. They wrote it after they had looked at a picture of a bird flying away from a tree.

The branches are bare.
The nest has lost its babies.
Bird, where do you fly?

Write like the Japanese

Write a *haiku.* Then make a magazine of poems and stories you have written. You can call it *Flower Basket* or *Hana Kago.* The words look like this—

Copy these Japanese characters on the cover of your magazine.

Japanese Customs in Texas

Then

The Japanese people who came to Texas long ago brought their customs with them. Here are some customs of Japanese families who lived in the Kishi Colony at Terry.

Bathing—Mr. Yoichi Norman Kishi grew up in Terry. He said, "Every family had a Japanese bath to relax their muscles. Our bath was in a bathhouse about ten feet away from our house. It was a wooden tub with a metal bottom. You would wash with soap and water and rinse off before you got in the tub. Then you stepped into the tub and sat down on a wooden platform. The water came up to your neck. It was very hot. There was a brick oven underneath the tub. We built a fire in the oven to heat the water.

"When I was young, it was my duty to prepare the bath for the family. Every day after I got home from school, I built the fire. I knew just how many sticks of wood to put on the fire. It took ten sticks to make the fire hot enough.

"It wasn't a chore I dreaded. I didn't have to watch the fire all the time. I could go off and play. Once in a while the fire would go out, and I would get a scolding."

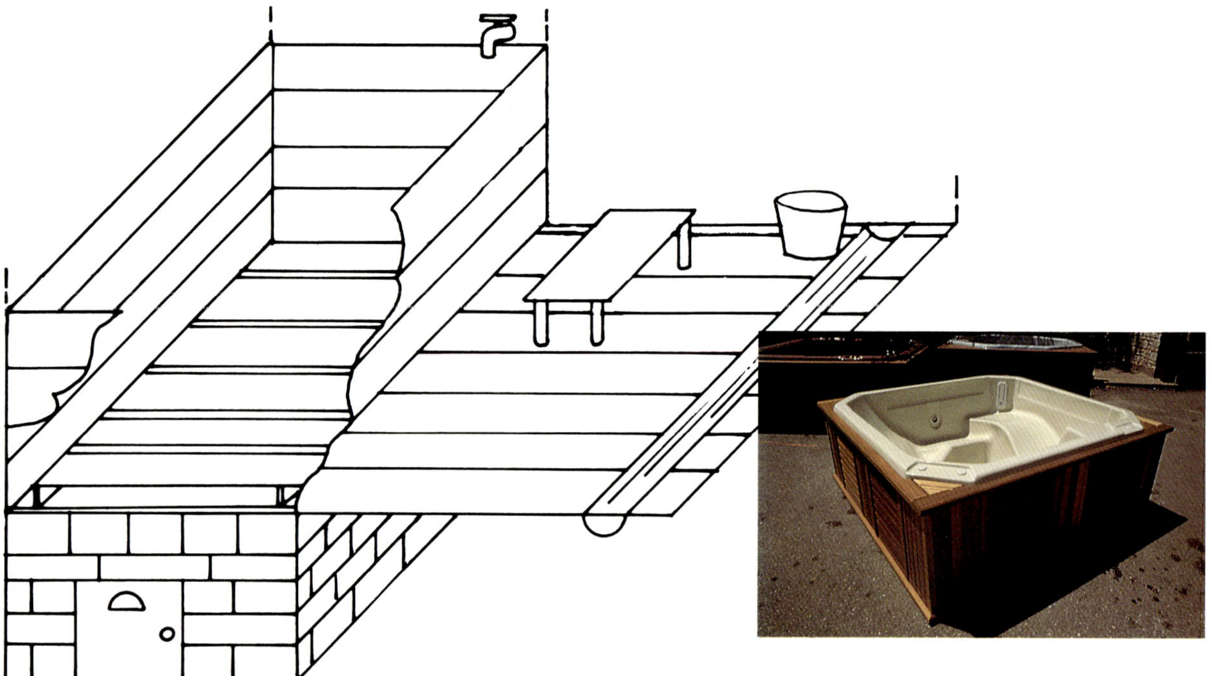

Eating – Rice, or *gohan,* was the main food of Japanese Texans. Soybeans were also important. The women made a cake out of soybean curds. They also ate fish and pickled vegetables. They drank green tea. Instead of forks, they used chopsticks, called *hashi.*

Clothing — People often wore straw sandals, called *zori*, outdoors. When they went inside, they left them at the door. This kept the floors nice and clean.

Now

Most of these customs are no longer kept by the Japanese Texans. They eat many of the same foods as other Texans. They wear the same kinds of clothes Texans wear, and they speak like other Texans.

Today, there is trade between the United States and Japan. Texans buy Japanese cars, computers, and stereos. Many Texans like products which are similar to things the early Japanese Texans used. You can find *zori*, *tofu*, or soybean curds, and hot tubs in many stores in Texas.

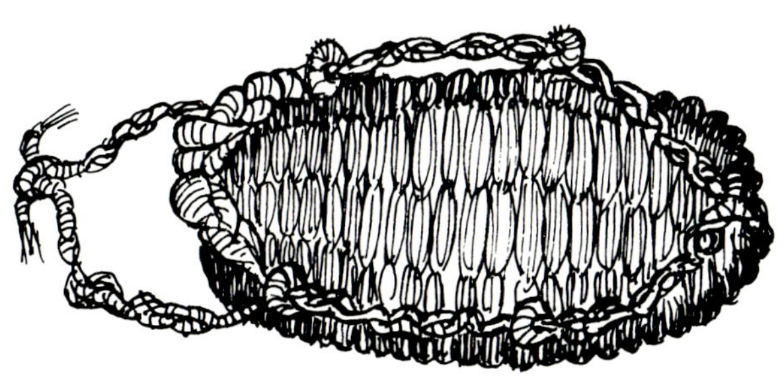

Make a Montage

How many Japanese products can you identify? How many cars have Japanese names? Collect pictures from magazines and newspapers. Draw other products. Make a montage from the pictures.

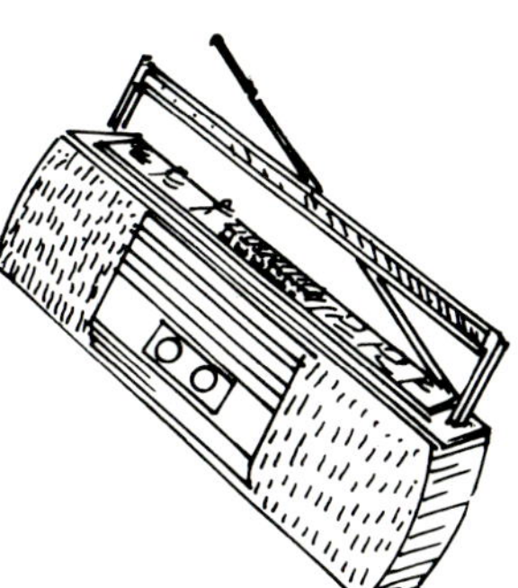

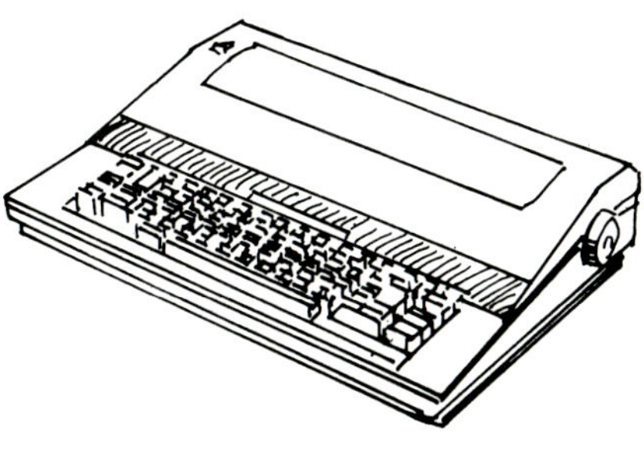

Mr. Taniguchi's Gift

AN OLD JAPANESE CUSTOM IS GIVING a gift to a person whom you visit. The custom is called *o-mi-ya-ge.* Many Japanese who came to Texas long ago practiced this custom. Mr. Isamu Taniguchi came to the United States in 1914 and now lives in Austin. He gave his city a special gift that took him 18 months to make. This gift was a garden that covers three acres. He finished the garden when he was 71 years old.

The Garden

Mr. Taniguchi's garden is different from an American garden. There aren't many flowers. It has trees and bushes and streams and ponds. There are large rocks lining the paths, and there are rocks in the garden. Mr. Taniguchi placed every rock himself. He also built a waterfall and a bridge called "The bridge-to-walk-over-the-moon." The bridge goes over a pond in which you can see the moon at night. Mr. Taniguchi said, "As you move, the moon follows, crossing over the water."

In the garden are many Japanese cherry trees. The garden is full of color when the trees bloom in the spring.

Peace

Mr. Taniguchi says that his garden stands for world peace. He wants the people of the world to live together in peace like the stones, plants, and water are together in his garden.

He likes children to visit the garden. He made it for them. Today they skip on the stones. Tomorrow he hopes they will be the keepers of peace.

You might like to visit Zilker Park and walk through Mr. Taniguchi's garden.

Play a Chopsticks Game

Japanese-Texan children played this game in a Houston park not too long ago. They were attending a family picnic of the Japanese American Citizens League. Two teams ran relays. They held pieces of popcorn with chopsticks as they ran. Try it. Learn how to hold chopsticks. Not all of the children at the picnic knew how to hold chopsticks. They had to learn too.

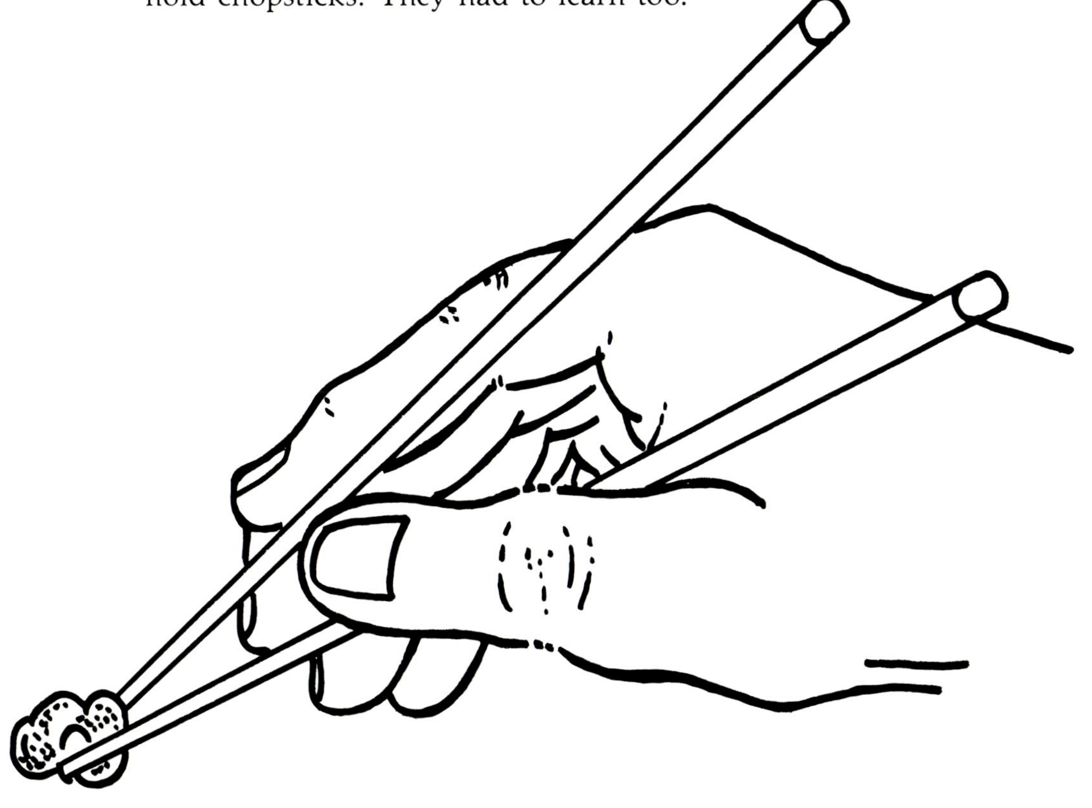

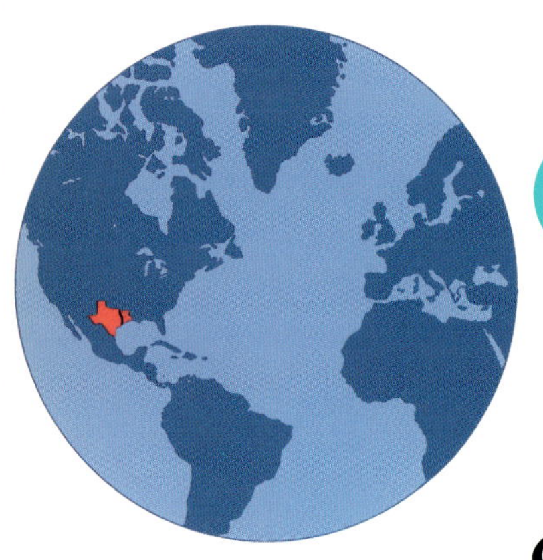

Cajun Texans

SHORTLY AFTER 1900, CAJUNS CAME to east Texas from Louisiana to find work. They came in great numbers to work in the oil business. Others became shrimp fishermen and farmers. Today, there are many Cajuns in east Texas.

The Cajuns brought their customs with them from Louisiana. They brought their language, which was Cajun French. They brought their foods, their music, and their stories. Texas Cajuns call Louisiana "the Old Country" and often go back there to visit.

A Cajun-Texan Tall Tale

THE CAJUNS ARE GREAT storytellers. Some of the stories, like the stories of their history, are mostly true. Others they tell for fun. We call stories that couldn't be true "tall tales." Here is a tall tale that the Cajuns tell about coming to Texas.

> A long time ago, a Cajun from Louisiana walked to Texas to find a job. He had a wooden peg leg. The ground was muddy, and the peg leg made holes in it. They looked like the holes that crawfish make in the mud. Now, Cajuns like to eat crawfish, so a bunch of them followed those holes all the way to Texas, looking for the crawfish. And that's how Cajuns got to Texas.

Cajuns love to tell stories like this one. Their life was not always funny, but if they could laugh, it did not seem so hard.

From France to Louisiana

THE REAL STORY OF THE CAJUNS is a sad one. Almost 400 years ago, many people from France sailed to Canada on ships. They settled near the sea and named their new land Acadia. These people called themselves Acadians. They spoke French, the language of France.

The English-speaking people in Canada did not want the Acadians to be there. They put them on ships and sent them away. Many of them became ill and died. Families were separated.

Many Acadians came to Louisiana, which had already been settled by French people. The Acadians settled along the coast. They had no money or belongings. For food they caught animals and fish. They gathered moss from the trees to stuff mattresses and to fill the cracks in their log homes. Later they planted fields of rice and corn, sugarcane and cotton.

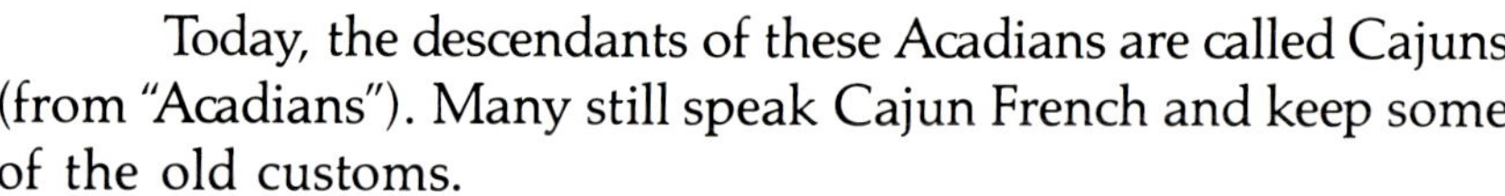

Today, the descendants of these Acadians are called Cajuns (from "Acadians"). Many still speak Cajun French and keep some of the old customs.

A Cajun Texan's Story

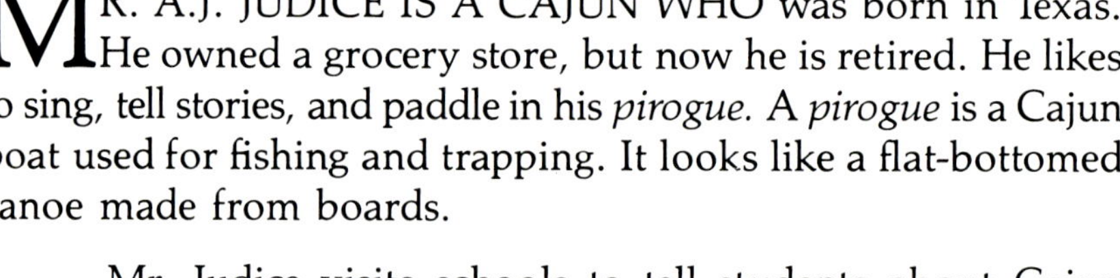

MR. A.J. JUDICE IS A CAJUN WHO was born in Texas. He owned a grocery store, but now he is retired. He likes to sing, tell stories, and paddle in his *pirogue.* A *pirogue* is a Cajun boat used for fishing and trapping. It looks like a flat-bottomed canoe made from boards.

Mr. Judice visits schools to tell students about Cajun customs. He teaches them how to play a "ting-a-ling" – a metal triangle – and tells them about Cajun music.

Cajun Music

"Every Saturday night we used to go to a different house for a party. The whole family went. We had a little band and sang and played music. The party was called a *fais do-do.* That's French baby talk for 'go to sleep.'

"The babies were put to bed in a back room. Then the band would play. Someone might have a fiddle or a washboard. They'd use anything that made music. Kids would keep time to the music with a ting-a-ling."

Long ago, the Acadians didn't bring musical instruments from Canada, so they made their own. They carved fiddles out of pieces of wood. They hit spoons together or rubbed them on washboards. For the triangles, they bent the tines of a hay fork. Sometimes they made a bass fiddle from a washtub, a broom handle, and a piece of cord.

Now Cajun bands have accordions and electric guitars. However, they haven't forgotten their "old-time" music. Cajuns love to dance and sing and have a good time. They say *"Laissez les bons temps roulez"* – "Let the good times roll."

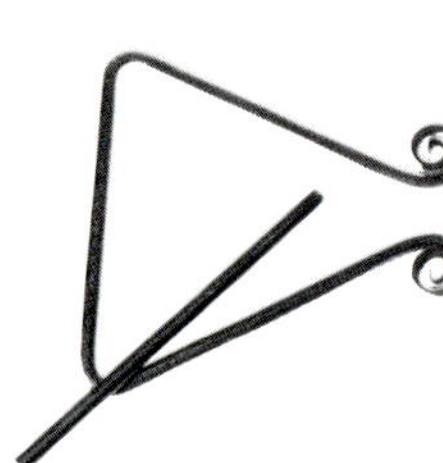

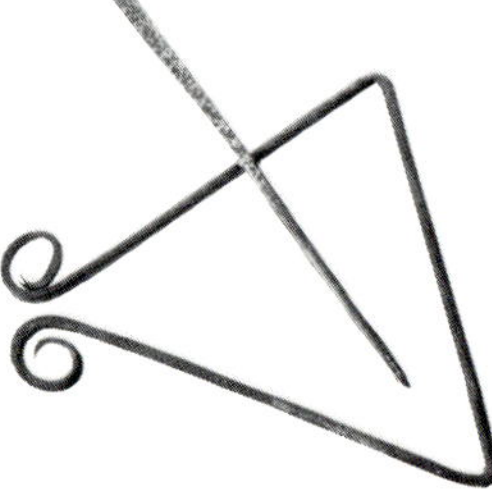

Have a Cajun Party

First, put together a band. Take some ideas from the Cajuns, and add some of your own. Find a washboard. Wrap tissue paper around a comb. Fill bottles with different amounts of water. Glue sandpaper to wooden blocks. Put pebbles in a can. Make up some new instruments.

Have a *fais do-do* party. Sing some of your favorite songs, while you play your instruments. "Let the good times roll."

Cajun Food

MR. JUDICE TALKED about Cajun food too. "Cajun cooking came from making use of everything they could eat: Crawfish, alligators, frogs that lived in the ditches." Joking, he said, "A Cajun will eat anything that doesn't eat him first."

Here are foods that Cajuns like to eat:

Rice is eaten at almost every meal. Many Cajun dishes are served over rice.

Boudin is a white sausage that is made with rice and ground pork.

Crawfish are small shellfish with two large claws. They are found in creeks, ponds, and ditches. Cajuns use them in many of their dishes.

Gumbo is a thick soup usually made with seafood or chicken and tomatoes, okra, spices, and peppers.

Peppers are small vegetables that are usually hot and spicy. Cajuns grow peppers and season their food with them.

Cajun mothers teach their daughters to cook, and Cajun fathers teach their sons to cook. Cajun men are good cooks and proud of it! They make gumbo and use lots of hot peppers! Cajuns like their food spicy!

Cajuns and Crawfish

MANY EAST TEXAS CAJUNS caught crawfish when they were young. Mr. "Tee Bruce" Broussard is one of these Cajuns. He said,

"We used to catch crawfish in the ponds. We cut up two tow sacks, and we sewed them together to make one wide one. Then we fastened it to two poles and pulled it through a pond. One of us stayed on shore, and the other stayed in the pond, his head just above water. We pulled it through the pond, keeping it close to the bottom to catch the crawfish. Then we heated water in a syrup can in the alley behind the house. We boiled the crawfish and then popped the tails. We ate them any time like a snack.

"My grandfather told me this story about crawfish.

" 'Did you know that the crawfish is the bravest creature alive? If you put an eagle and a crawfish on a railroad track, when a train comes, the eagle will fly away, but the crawfish will put up his claws and try to catch it!' "

Can you top this Cajun tall tale?

Tell a Tall Tale

Have you ever told a tall tale? If not, ask your family and friends to tell you some. Then, make up one of your own. Tell your tale to a friend – the taller the tale, the better!

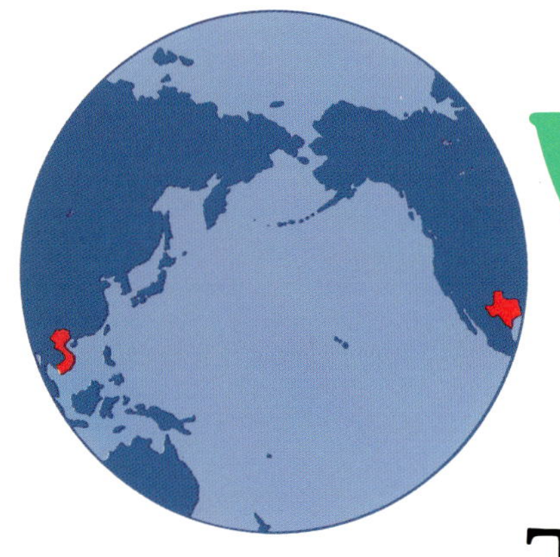

Vietnamese Texans

THE VIETNAMESE PEOPLE ARE NEWCOMERS to Texas. The first big group came in 1975 after the Vietnam War. Many of them were airlifted from Vietnam to the United States.

Later, more and more people left Vietnam. They were afraid of the new government and wanted freedom. Many left in small, leaky boats. They had to leave most of their belongings behind. Some people were robbed and beaten by pirates. Thousands died on the boats or drowned when the boats sank. Others went without food for many days before they were rescued or reached land.

Today, many thousands of these Vietnamese people live in Texas. Most of them live in cities or on the Texas coast. Some of them are fishermen, as they were in Vietnam.

Starting Over

IT IS NOT EASY FOR PEOPLE TO BEGIN a new life in another country. The language and the customs are often very different. The Vietnamese people had problems when they reached Texas. Not many of them could speak English. It was hard to find work. They did not know the laws.

Groups of people from cities and churches and schools helped the Vietnamese. They helped them find places to live. They taught them how to use American washing machines and stoves. They helped them learn English.

The Vietnamese people were eager to learn. Some of the Vietnamese who came first helped teach those who came later. Many of these early arrivals have become United States citizens. They are now Vietnamese Americans.

This Laotian girl is learning English as a Second Language in a San Antonio school. Many people from Laos and Cambodia, as well as Vietnam, have come to live in Texas in recent years.

Vietnamese Texans from Houston

MR. KHOI TIEN BUI WAS A government leader and a poet in Vietnam. In Houston he helps Vietnamese refugees. His program has helped thousands of Vietnamese people make new homes for themselves in Houston. Mr. Bui now writes poems in English. He wants to share his feelings about his new country.

Vietnamese Refugees in America

The Vietnam refugee
What does he bring to American room?
A rose planting itself on the rock
and learning to bloom. . . .

Mr. Nam Nelson Phung also works in the refugee program. He was a teacher in Vietnam. Now he helps the Vietnamese people learn about living in an American city. He gives advice to them and helps them with English.

Mr. Phung wants Americans to know about Vietnamese Texans. "The family is very important to Vietnamese people," Mr. Phung said. "To honor the parents is most important. I would try to be first in my class to honor my parents. I played soccer in Vietnam when I was a kid. I would try my hardest to make a goal to honor my parents too.

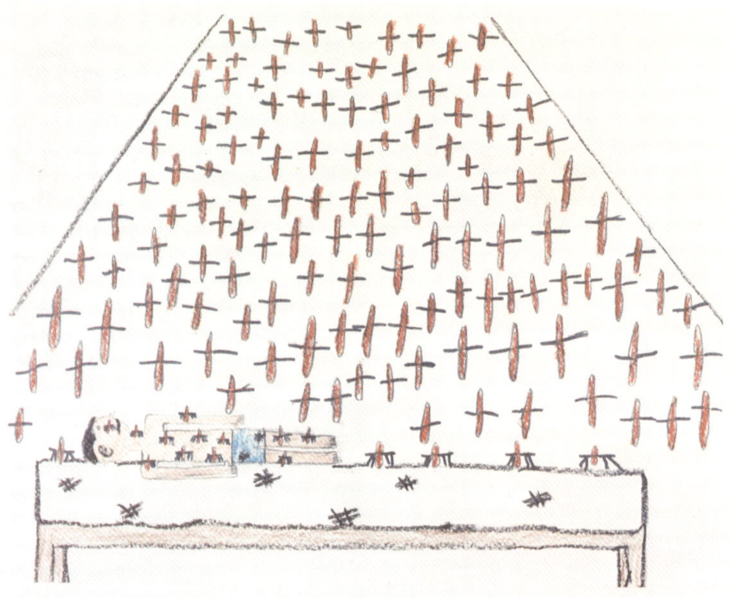

"Children help their parents. We tell a legend to explain how we feel. A son wanted to take care of his parents. They were very poor and didn't have a mosquito net to cover their bed. The son lay down on the bed first, so all the mosquitoes would bite him. Then, when his parents went to bed, the mosquitoes were gone. The parents could sleep without being bitten."

And from San Antonio!

Viet and Troy

Viet was three years old and his brother, Troy, was nine months old when they left Vietnam. Their father was a pilot in Vietnam, and he flew his family out of the country. Now he has a restaurant and take-out food business in San Antonio. Viet and Troy are teenagers. They work at the restaurant after school. At night, they often study in one of the bright red booths. Viet said, "Since we came from another country and had to start all over with nothing, we can see that hard work can get you somewhere."

The boys talked about life in a Vietnamese-American family. Troy said, "We have a lot of discipline in the family. It's . . . very strict. My dad doesn't want us to walk alone." Viet added, "There's a lot of respect for grown-ups and other relatives older than you. There's not any talking back."

Troy spoke next. "We get together with our relatives on holidays like the New Year and over the weekends. We celebrate on the Vietnamese New Year. We have a family gathering. It's sort of like Thanksgiving. We prepare food. We have fruits and meats that we give to our ancestors, who are dead, and we say [prayers] for their spirits to come down to earth to eat the food. And we have a candle that we light, and, when it comes to the bottom and the candle is gone, we know that the spirit is gone. After that, we eat the food, and Dad tells us about our ancestors."

Patrick and Jo

Patrick and Jo work in their father's store. The store is on a street in northeast San Antonio. About 25 Vietnamese families live on the two streets in this area. The families saved money to buy a little house to use as a Buddhist temple. The temple is on the street behind the store. Jo's mother often makes meals without meat to serve at the temple.

The store is full of all sorts of things. There is Vietnamese clothing, like sandals and *aố dāi*. *Aố dāi* are dresses with high collars, long sleeves, and slits up the sides. They are worn with

long pants. Tapes of Vietnamese music are for sale. There are cooking pots and rice bowls. Seventeen different brands of *nuoc mam,* or fish sauce, are stacked on the shelves. There are fresh shrimp in coolers, bean sprouts in sacks, and all kinds of rice noodles and teas. Shoppers listen to music and talk. They can pick up a free Vietnamese-language newspaper. It is full of news about Vietnamese people in Austin and San Antonio.

Patrick talked about foods that Vietnamese Texans like. He said, "We sell a lot of fish sauce. We put it on everything, like ketchup. We use it instead of salt.

"Rice is the main food. We sell a lot of rice and rice noodles and bean sprouts. We make a soup with rice and noodles and pork bone and bean sprouts and other vegetables in it. You can put anything in the soup. We often eat it at lunch."

Patrick is in college now. He came from Vietnam when he was 14. He played some games in Vietnam that the children on his street also play.

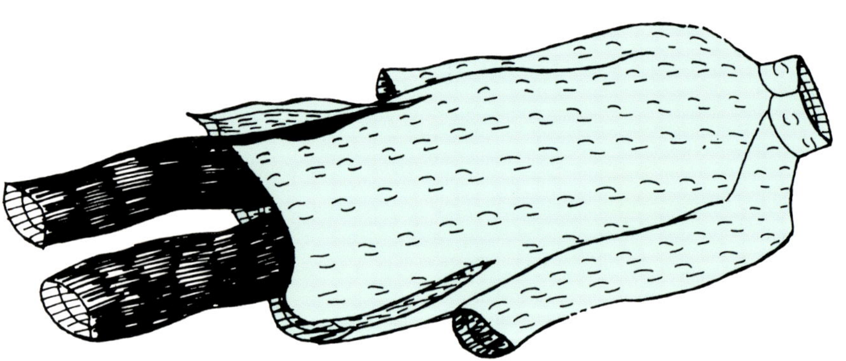

Play a Vietnamese Game

One of the games Patrick played is called *chọi đồng tiền,* or tossing the coin. It may be played with any number of people. Here is one way to play the game. Draw a line in the dirt. Stand a few feet away and throw a coin at the line. If your coin crosses the line, you are out. If your coin is the closest one to the line, you are the winner.

Jo is a high school student. She talked about the candles, sticks of incense, and fancy red papers that are for sale in the store. "They are for altars. Many Vietnamese families have an altar in their homes. On the death days of their ancestors, they burn incense. And they burn papers with messages on them to go up to the spirits." Jo said, "We do it on the death days of our grandparents and at Tết, the Lunar New Year."

Remembering Celebrations

VIETNAMESE-TEXAN ADULTS DO NOT WANT their children to forget the important customs of Vietnam. There are groups in Houston and San Antonio which plan celebrations for the Vietnamese people. They celebrate Tết (the Lunar New Year) and Trung Thu.

Trung Thu is a children's festival. In Vietnam, it was celebrated at the end of the rice harvest. This is the time of the biggest full moon of the year. Sometimes Trung Thu is called the Mid-Autumn Festival.

Children receive gifts of paper lanterns shaped like animals or stars. They eat moon cakes, which are round rice cakes filled with sweets. The night is bright with the light of lanterns as the full moon rises. The children sing songs, and sometimes there is a children's parade.

Mr. Bui wrote a poem about Trung Thu. Here's part of it.

The moon party with laughter and shout
Happy time! You better watch out!

Lanterns in their hands, children sing.
The beautiful moon. I wonder what does it bring?

Make a Scrapbook

Here is a newspaper story about a Vietnamese celebration in San Antonio. Newspapers and magazines often carry stories about Texan cultures.

Find pictures and articles like this one. Put them in a scrapbook.

Vietnamese holiday focuses on children

By PAULA TRAN
SPECIAL TO THE EXPRESS-NEWS

A full moon will light the way Saturday night for San Antonio's Vie[...]
sters as the[...]
some 50 br[...]
handmade la[...]
brate their a[...]
New Year, Te[...]

Sponsored by [...]
etnamese Com[...]
brated at Our La[...]
lic Church, 223 E[...]
Mid-Autumn Fes[...]
the Vietnamese c[...]

The 7:30 p.m.[...]
the traditional dr[...]
bition of martial [...]
etnamese folk s[...]
highlight of the [...]
dren's parade an[...]
terns.

Lanterns ha[...]

Preparations f[...]
festival began m[...]
ago with the ted[...]
the cellophane-c[...]
terns by the 20 n[...]
namese Student [...]
University of Te[...]

"The lanterns [...]
— a star, an a[...]
moon," explains [...]
dent Thuy Than[...]
lem, of course, is [...]
reeds thinly enou[...]
But the delight c[...]
joy in the festiva[...]
work."

In the past week, however, activities have accelerated to a feverish pitch. Proud mothers sewed the customary new "ao dai," or long dresses, for their children and baked "mooncakes" and other delicacies [...]

grant from Vietnam, recounts this most commonly accepted version which will be presented once again during the festivities.

[...]ther clarify the significance [...]namese high holiday of the [...]g, president of the [...] Association, ana[...] [...]ymbols associated

[...]ake are being pre[...] [...]emony — a flat [...]senting the Earth [...]d one, symbolic [...]

[...]ese 'mooncak[...] [...]s of private co[...] the peasants w[...] [...]ppressed by a[...]

[...]hat the holida[...] [...]ng explains it [...]y's historic s[...] [...]ur heritage, [...]ever can be [...] from Vietna[...] [...]ultural life."

[...]ous

[...]nally des[...] [...]ition, the [...] find mor[...] [...]t cousin, [...]for child[...] process[...] [...]rit of th[...] [...]n of the [...] being r[...] [...]nilated [...]an sc[...] [...]old-wo[...] to pr[...] [...]ion o[...] fore[...]

Vietnamese youngsters select lanterns for their New Year's parade. They are Hong Tran, 9; Jacqueline Hoang, 2; Jason Tran, 2; and Hang Tran, 13.

Photo by JOHNNY GARZA

Salute to Other Texan Cultures

ALL TEXANS ARE DESCENDED FROM people who came from somewhere else. Where did your ancestors come from? Maybe they came from several different countries. Are these cultural groups represented in *Texans: A Story of Texan Cultures for Young People*?

Many groups have made Texas what it is today. We would like to tell the stories of all the other cultures. You can write a new chapter. Salute another Texan culture. Then you can add your chapter to this book.

Write about a Texan Culture

Select a group, perhaps one that you come from. Study chapters from *Texans* for ideas of what to write about. Collect information from newspapers, magazines, books, and filmstrips. Best of all, talk to Texans who are from that group and ask them questions.

You can write your chapter as an article or as the story of a make-believe person. You can include recipes, directions for games, or songs. Take some photographs. Draw pictures. Make up some things to do.

Share your chapter with others, and don't forget to send a copy to The Institute of Texan Cultures!

The Naturalization Ceremony

THE U.S. GOVERNMENT regularly holds naturalization ceremonies, in which immigrants from all over the world become citizens of the United States. Almost every month, one of these ceremonies is held at The Institute of Texan Cultures in San Antonio. During a recent naturalization ceremony, 184 men and women who now live in Texas became citizens. These people had come from 38 different countries. A man from India wearing a turban sat next to a lady from Finland. Their homelands were thousands of miles apart. Here they stood together as they repeated the oath of citizenship to their new country.

These newcomers bring their beliefs and their stories with them to Texas. They share their customs with their neighbors and friends. In this way, Texan cultures grow and become richer year by year.

Texans and the World

IN THIS BOOK YOU HAVE READ stories of many Texans. Now you can begin to see what a rich heritage we Texans share.

Think of the many customs that were brought here by the immigrants. These customs have become part of our Texas way of life. Eating sausage, breaking *piñatas* at parties, trimming Christmas trees: These customs came from other countries. Words like "kindergarten," "okra," and "rodeo" came from other languages. Our religions were brought from far away. Much of our music and art comes from other places.

Texans have celebrations to honor and share these customs. Every year, many cultural groups in Texas have festivals, and everyone is invited. There are parades, like the Juneteenth parades, the Mexican Independence Day parades, and the St. Patrick's Day parades. At the Lunar New Year, Asian Texans perform dragon and lion dances. They serve their foods and demonstrate their arts and crafts. And the Texas Folklife Festival celebrates many, many Texan cultures.

The whole world is here.

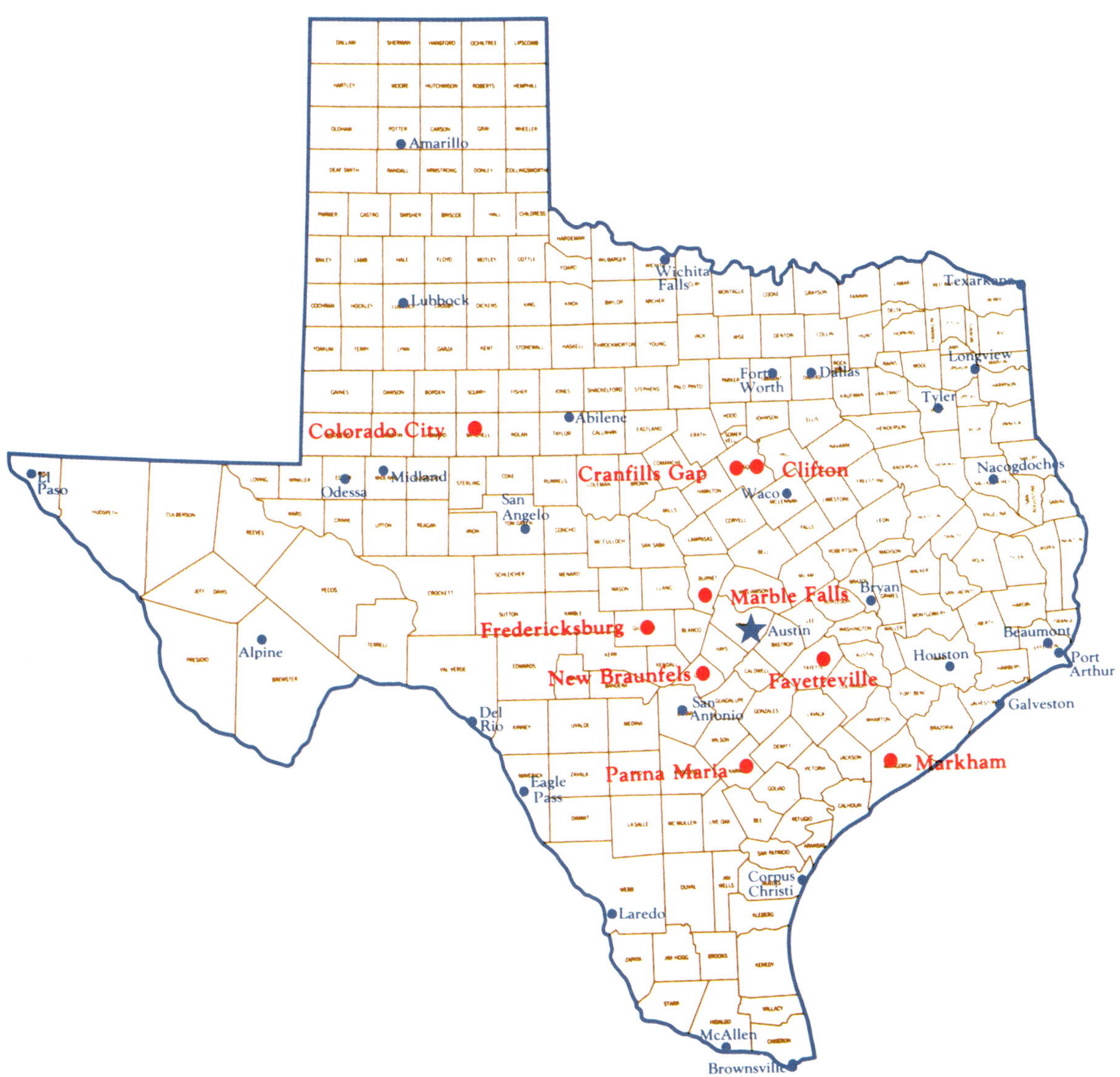
Amarillo
Lubbock
Wichita Falls
Texarkana
Longview
Fort Worth
Dallas
Tyler
Abilene
Colorado City
El Paso
Odessa
Midland
Cranfills Gap
Clifton
Waco
Nacogdoches
San Angelo
Marble Falls
Bryan
Fredericksburg
Austin
Beaumont
Houston
Port Arthur
New Braunfels
Fayetteville
Alpine
Galveston
San Antonio
Del Rio
Markham
Panna Maria
Eagle Pass
Corpus Christi
Laredo
McAllen
Brownsville

Index

Acknowledgments

This book is the child of many people. First of all, Bonnie Truax, Director of Educational Programs at The Institute of Texan Cultures, saw this project through from its beginnings, reading, advising, and offering valuable insights along the way. Second, Dr. James C. McNutt, ITC Director of Research, also followed its progress, providing assistance and expertise.

The following people helped in the creation of *Texans* with their stories, their knowledge, their efforts in locating people, pictures, and artifacts, and their caring attention.

Norma Bradley Allen, Anna Anes, Emily Anes, Ruth Seele Aniol, Gil Baca, Pat Blattman, Hettye Wallace Branch, Phyllis Braverman, John Loyd Broussard, Rosemary Birowicz Bryant, Khoi Tien Bui, Rosa Carrillo, Georgia Carson, John Carson, Penelope Carson, Rosemary Catacalos, Sheridan D. Cavitt Jr., Clarence Colwick, Irv Dubrin, Bob Henry Duckens, Willie O. Duckens, Kay Kohara Edwards, Leah Fillis, Maria Garczynski, Sr. Alexandrine Gieniec, Alice Goldsmith, Mikoko K. Gorup, Valerie Juszczyk Grace, William Guardia, P. Jack Henson, Clyde Hester, Rev. John M. Homerstad, Joshua Houtkin, Lily Houtkin, Janice Huey, Mary Jendrush, Camilla Jenson, Rev. Lawrence C. Jenson, A.J. Judice, Fr. John Kaloudis, Rick Kalwoda, Stefania Karpowicz, John W. Keineburg, Jane Keller, Alma Key, Ruby Kirton, Norman Kishi, Mattie Knudson, May Lam, Sylvia Laznovsky, Ruth Lew, Mabel Bryant Leyda, Sophie Lin, Peg Litherbury, Cathy Liu, Leslie Liu, Tina Liu, Teresa McClure, Holland McCombs, Raymond McCumba III, Roberta McGregor, Esther MacMillan, Sophie Madalinski, Rae Mangos, Teri (Teruyo) Matsuoka, Dr. Fred R. von der Mehden, Daniel Mendoza, Mary Mika, Dr. Sigrid Moe, Gladys Moryl, Esther Muñoz, Dominic Netek, Mabel Noble, Mary Colwick Orbeck, Steve Pao, Linda Peterson, Nam Nelson Phung, Troy Phung, Viet Phung, Aaronetta Pierce, Thalia Plomarity, Dorothy Redus Robinson, Ann Rogers, Ada Mae Rohne, Sydney Sako, Melvin Sance Jr., Christian Schmidt, Helen Slattery, Helen Stanley, Claude Stanush, Dr. Alan Taniguchi, Isamu Taniguchi, Eva Templeton, Jo Thai, Patrick Thai, Chinh Tran, Paula Tran, Nina Usick, Dr. Alvia Wardlaw, Sharlotte Washington, Selma Weiner, Bettye N. White, Alicia F. Wilson, Emilie Wofford, Virginia Y. Wong, Ann Worswick, Jody Wright, and Esther Wu.

The following individuals provided invaluable assistance as readers of the manuscript.

Dr. Francis E. Abernethy, Dr. Alwyn Barr, Pat Blattman, Georgia Carson, Jackie Christenson, Kay Kohara Edwards, Madeleine Grmela, William Guardia, Dr. Thomas H. Guderjan, P. Jack Henson, Dr. Thomas R. Hester, Dr. Gilberto M. Hinojosa, A.J. Judice, Fr. John Kaloudis, James Patrick McGuire, Dr. Clinton Machann, Dr. Marian L. Martinello, Dr. Fred R. von der Mehden, Dr. W.W. Newcomb Jr., Jane Parker, Dr. Peter L. Petersen, Dr. Gerald E. Poyo, Melvin Sance Jr., Rabbi Samuel M. Stahl, Thomas K. Walls, Dr. Bobby Weaver, Alicia F. Wilson, and Virginia Y. Wong.

To all of you, and to the staff of The Institute of Texan Cultures, I extend my profound thanks and share with you *Texans: A Story of Texan Cultures for Young People.* This is *our* story.

– B.E.S.

Sources

Immigration

Hewgley, Breathett S. Oral history, Institute of Texan Cultures, San Antonio, June 11, 1981.

Personal correspondence from Christine Hinderlie Reinertsen of Oslo, Texas, February 1, 1932, to Camilla Jenson in Clifton, Texas, concerning voyage of 1884.

Indian Texans

Kirkland, Forrest (paintings), and W.W. Newcomb Jr. (text). *The Rock Art of Texas Indians.* Austin: University of Texas Press, 1967.

San Antonio Museum Association (slides of Indian rock art).

Griffith, William Joyce. *The Hasinai Indians of East Texas as Seen by Europeans, 1687-1772.* Philological and Documentary Studies II, no. 3. New Orleans: Middle American Research Institute, Tulane University, 1954.

The Melting Pot: Ethnic Cuisine in Texas (Indian corn soup recipe). Rev. ed. San Antonio: Institute of Texan Cultures, 1983.

Densmore, Frances. "The Alabama Indians and Their Music" (corn dance song). *Straight Texas.* Ed. J. Frank Dobie and Mody C. Boatright. Texas Folklore Society Publication XIII. Austin: Steck Company, 1937.

Spanish Texans

Santos, Richard G. *Aguayo Expedition into Texas, 1721: An Annotated Translation of the Five Versions of the Diary Kept by Br. Juan Antonio de la Peña* (entry for March 27, 1721). Austin: Jenkins Publishing Co., 1981.

Kress, Margaret Kenney, tr. "Diary of Fray Gaspar José de Solís, in the Year 1767-68." *Southwestern Historical Quarterly* XXXV, July 1931.

Jaxon (Jack Jackson). Manuscript map, "San Antonio de Béxar." 1981.

MacMillan, Esther. Chapter IV, "The People of San Antonio, Part II" (trans. of will of Maria Betancour, 1779, Bexar Archives). *San Antonio in the Eighteenth Century.* San Antonio: San Antonio Bicentennial Heritage Committee, 1976.

Weddle, Robert S., and Robert H. Thonhoff. *Drama and Conflict: The Texas Saga of 1776* (Governor Ripperda's papers). Austin: Madrona Press, Inc., 1976.

Cook, Sr. Gertrude, and Esther MacMillan. Chapter VII, "San Antonio in 1776" (laws). *San Antonio in the Eighteenth Century.* San Antonio: San Antonio Bicentennial Heritage Committee, 1976.

Jackson, Jack. *Los Mesteños: Spanish Ranching in Texas* (brands). College Station: Texas A&M University Press, 1986.

Anglo-American Texans

Cavitt, Ellen Burnett. "Some Tracings of Cavett-Cavitt Family History, 1725-1965" (Ann Cavitt's journal). Unpublished.

Cooper, Patricia, and Norma Bradley Buferd. *The Quilters: Women and Domestic Art* (oral history). Garden City: Doubleday & Company, Inc., 1977.

Smithwick, Noah. *The Evolution of a State or Recollections of Old Texas Days.* Austin: Gammel Book Company, 1900; reprint, Austin: University of Texas Press, 1983.

Vance, Silas W. "Life and Leisure at Lucky Ridge." *The Folklore of Texan Cultures.* Ed. Francis Edward Abernethy. Texas Folklore Society Publication XXXVIII. Austin: Encino Press, 1974.

Afro-American Texans

Thomas, Loydean. "Family reunited in song" (quote from Willie O. Duckens). San Antonio *Express-News,* Aug. 3, 1985.

Branch, Hettye Wallace. *The Story of "80 John."* New York: Greenwich Book Publishers, Inc., 1960.

Robinson, Dorothy Redus. *The Bell Rings at Four: A Black Teacher's Chronicle of Change.* Austin: Madrona Press, Inc., 1978.

Michels, Barbara, and Bettye White. *Apples on a Stick: The Folklore of Black Children.* New York: Coward-McCann, Inc., 1983.

Mexican Texans

Los Cuentitos de la Señora Mendoza. (Unpublished.) Carvajal Elementary School, San Antonio.

Jimenez, Leonardo "Flaco." Oral history, Institute of Texan Cultures, San Antonio, May 28, 1986.

German Texans

Seele, Hermann. *The Cypress and Other Writings of a German Pioneer in Texas.* Tr. Edward C. Breitenkamp. Austin: University of Texas Press, 1979.

Jordan, Gilbert J. *German Texana: A Bilingual Collection of Traditional Materials.* Burnet: Eakin Press, 1980.

Eiband, Laura. Oral history, Sophienburg Museum and Archives, New Braunfels, April 27, 1977.

Polish Texans

Baker, T. Lindsay. *The Polish Texans.* San Antonio: Institute of Texan Cultures, 1982.

Stanush, Mary Burda. Oral history, Institute of Texan Cultures, San Antonio, September 11, 1984.

Czech Texans

Machann, Clinton, and James W. Mendl. *Krásňa Amerika: A Study of the Texas Czechs, 1851-1939.* Austin: Eakin Press, 1983.

Baca, Marie. *Memorial Book of Recipes.* Taylor: Merchants Press, 1957.

Pazdral, Olga J. "Czech Folklore in Texas." M.A. thesis, University of Texas, Austin, 1942.

Věstník (SPJST Herald), Temple, Texas, January 15, 1986.

Norwegian Texans

Pierson, Oris Emerald. *Norwegian Settlements in Bosque County, Texas.* Clifton: Bosque Memorial Museum, 1979.

Rohne, Chris L., and LaVerne Pendleton. "The History of Cranfills Gap, Texas." Cranfills Gap Chapter of Young Homemakers of Texas, December 1975.

Jewish Texans

Nathan, Anne, and Harry I. Cohen. *The Man Who Stayed in Texas: The Life of Rabbi Henry Cohen.* New York: McGraw-Hill Book Company, Inc., Whittlesey House, 1941.

Marinbach, Bernard. *Galveston: Ellis Island of the West.* Albany: State University of New York Press, 1983.

Japanese Texans

Kurosawa, Kiyoko Tanabe. "Seito Saibara's Diary of Planting a Japanese Colony in Texas." *Hitotsubashi Journal of Social Studies* II, no. 1 (August 1964).

Tanabe, Kiyoko. "The Japanese Immigrant in the Houston-Harris County Area." M.A. thesis, Rice Institute, Houston, 1956.

Wingate, Gwendolyn. "The Kishi Colony." *The Folklore of Texan Cultures.* Ed. Francis Edward Abernethy. Texas Folklore Society Publication XXXVIII. Austin: Encino Press, 1974.

Norman Kishi, Canyon Lake (sketch of bathtub).

Walls, Thomas K. *The Japanese Texans* (game). San Antonio: Institute of Texan Cultures, 1987.

Cajun Texans

Rushton, William Faulkner. *The Cajuns: From Acadia to Louisiana.* New York: Farrar Straus Giroux, 1979.

Vietnamese Texans

Von der Mehden, Fred R. "Indochinese." *The Ethnic Groups of Houston.* Ed. Fred R. von der Mehden. Houston: Rice University Studies, 1984.

Bui-Tien-Khoi (Poet Laureate of Houston). "Vietnamese Refugees in America." *America, My First Feelings.* Privately published, 1981, 1983.

Khoi Tien Bui [anglicized order of name above]. "The Mid-Autumn Festival." Manuscript.

San Antonio *Express-News,* September 24, 1983, San Antonio.

Credits

Uncredited photographs are staff productions of The Institute of Texan Cultures. Uncredited drawings are by Jim Cosgrove, ITC staff.

Indian Texans 7: (knife) San Antonio Museum Association, San Antonio. 10: Detail of mural by Nola Montgomery, 1983. Caddoan Mounds State Historic Site, Texas Parks and Wildlife Department, Alto. 12: Reagan Bradshaw, Austin. 13: *t. Texas Highways* Magazine, Austin; *b.* Reagan Bradshaw, Austin.

Spanish Texans 15, 16: Drawings by José Cisneros. José Cisneros, *Riders Across the Centuries: Horsemen of the Spanish Borderlands* (El Paso: Texas Western Press of The University of Texas at El Paso, 1984). 18: (retablo) Daughters of the Republic of Texas, The Alamo, San Antonio. 19: J. Frank Dobie Collection, Iconography—Harry Ransom Humanities Research Center, University of Texas at Austin.

Anglo-American Texans 20: *t. Harper's New Monthly Magazine* (New York: Harper and Brothers, 1879), vol. 59. *b.* Holland McCombs, Wheelock. 22: Erwin E. Smith Collection, Amon Carter Museum, Fort Worth. 25: Painting by Clara McDonald Williamson, "A Day's Work Is Done," 1946. Amon Carter Museum, Fort Worth.

Afro-American Texans 29: Detail of mural by Dr. John Thomas Biggers, "Quilting Bee," 1981. Donated by Mr. and Mrs. S.M. McAshan. Houston Music Hall, Houston. Photo by Earlie Hudnall. 30: D. W. Wallace Estate, Loraine. 32, 34 *t.*: Dorothy Redus Robinson, Palestine. 35: *b. Texas Highways* Magazine, Austin.

Mexican Texans 36: Kathy Vargas, San Antonio. 37: Al Rendon, San Antonio. 39: *t.* Texas Folklife Resources. Photo by Pat Jasper, Austin; *m.* Texas Folklife Resources. Photo by Kathy Vargas, San Antonio; *b.* Texas Folklife Resources. Photo by Pat Jasper, Austin. 40, 41: Drawings by students of Carvajal Elementary School, San Antonio. Barbara Stanush collection.

German Texans 44: *Texas Highways* Magazine, Austin. 46: Sophienburg Museum and Archives, New Braunfels. 47: Texas Parks and Wildlife Department, Austin. 49: *Texas Highways* Magazine, Austin.

Polish Texans 51: Seraphic Sisters, Shrine of Our Lady of Czestochowa, San Antonio. 52: Barbara Stanush, San Antonio. 53, 54: Stan Garczynski, Houston. 55: *Texas Highways* Magazine, Austin.

Czech Texans 57: Wharton County Historical Museum, Wharton. 60: Gil Baca, Houston. 62: Sylvia Laznovsky, Ennis.

Norwegian Texans 66: Peter J. Rosendahl, cartoonist. *Decorah-Posten,* Decorah, Iowa. The Norwegian-American Museum, Decorah, Iowa. 68: *t., b.* John Homerstad, Temple. 69: *t.* Barbara Stanush, San Antonio; *b.* Bosque Memorial Museum, Clifton.

Chinese Texans 70: *Texas Highways* Magazine, Austin. 71: *World Journal,* Houston. 73: Drawing by Maria Mendez, Ogden Elementary School, San Antonio.

Jewish Texans 80: *t.* Rosella Werlin, Houston; *b.* Archives of Temple B'nai Israel, Galveston. 82: Abraham and Adaia Shumsky. *Alef-Bet, a Hebrew Primer* (New York: Union of American Hebrew Congregations, 1979).

Greek Texans 84: *Texas Highways* Magazine, Austin. 87: Drawing by Sandra Reyna, Rodriguez Elementary School, San Antonio. 88: *l., r.* Thalia Plomarity, Corpus Christi.

Japanese Texans 90: Kiyoaki Saibara Estate, Houston. 91: May, Julia, and Nina Onishi, Islington, Mass. 93: (calligraphy) Mikoko K. Gorup, San Antonio. 96: Barbara Stanush, San Antonio.

Cajun Texans 98: Drawing by Yanira Vegerano, Cotton Elementary School, San Antonio. 100: *t.* Randy Mallory, Tyler; *b.* Jay Elledge, Lafayette Natural History Museum, Lafayette, La. 101: Jay Elledge, Lafayette Natural History Museum, Lafayette, La. 102: *t.* Randy Mallory, Tyler; *b. Texas Highways* Magazine, Austin.

Vietnamese Texans 106: Drawing by Robbie Rodriguez, Colonies North Elementary School, San Antonio. 109: Lac Tran, San Antonio. 110: (Vietnamese painting) Chinh Tran, San Antonio.